CELEBRATING OUR L

This eclectic collection will hopefully have wide appeal and is, basically, things which, over many years of involvement with old motorcycles, intrigued me; people, places and, of course, the motorcycles. There's not a huge amount of rhyme nor reason, while I've plenty of other subjects to investigate in the future too.

Most of those featured in this collection I've had personal involvement with or experience of; I've been lucky enough to have ridden every incarnation of Bonneville, from the first pre-units to the latest 'modern' examples – in my humble opinion, the 'best' of the bunch was an extremely well sorted 1970 USA spec, which combined classic looks and agility with a fantastic, eager engine – several Vincent twins, many Bantams, a couple of Rotary Nortons, at least two Scotts, KTTs from Mk.I to Mk.VIII.

I don't pretend to be privileged enough to know either Jeff Smith or Geoff Duke, though I have met the former on several occasions and seen, first hand, his almost unbelievable skill as he hustled a sidecar outfit up the Healy Pass on the Irish National Rally, as I flailed around on a solo, unable to keep up, while the late Barry Sheene provided me with one of my most 'memorable' experiences (and earlier my favourite toy...); around 10 years ago, when I was helping out on *Classic Racer* magazine, Barry phoned from Australia asking to speak to my then editor, Nigel Clark, about a feature in the magazine. Nigel not being in, I took the call, only for Barry to explain he wasn't too impressed with a report we'd put in from the MotoGP support race at Donington. But rather than rant for ages, he simply played, in its entirety, Alanis Morissette's song You Learn featuring the line 'Swallow it down (what a jagged little pill)' down the phone and left it at that... it was only two days later that we learned of the illness which was eventually to claim him.

Cadwell Park is a place I've visited for years – one of my earliest memories is struggling up the hill to Cadwell in the family 2CV sometime in the early 1980s – and only 10 miles from where I've ended up living, while Brooklands is always a huge joy to visit – a walk up the banking is simply amazing, in that one doesn't appreciate just how steep it is, until trying to climb it – and my first blast up Test Hill was one of the more memorable moments of my motorcycling career.

The rockers' cultural movement is something I've only ever skirted around – ownership of a Brando-esque black leather jacket age 16 was more Ramones inspired than rocker revival – while I did have a seminal BSA cafe racer for a while, too.

So, there you have it, reasons for each and every chapter; yes, perhaps they are rather self-indulgent, but I do hope that others take pleasure and enjoyment from it too. I've always reasoned that if I'm interested in something then others will be too (well, it always seems to be the case when I'm trying to buy something!) so, on that reckoning, I won't be apologetic about my selections, just say – I hope you enjoy what we've put together.

James.

EDITOR
James Robinson
Tel 01507 529405 Fax 01507 529495
email jrobinson@mortons.co.uk

GROUP EDITOR
Steve Rose

GROUP PRODUCTION EDITOR
Tim Hartley

DESIGNER
Michael Baumber

DIVISIONAL ADVERTISING MANAGER
David England
email dengland@mortons.co.uk

ADVERTISING
Dawn Clay
Tel 01507 524004
email dclay@mortons.co.uk

SUBSCRIPTION MANAGER
Paul Deacon
CIRCULATION MANAGER
Steve O'Hara
MARKETING MANAGER
Charlotte Park
PRODUCTION MANAGER
Craig Lamb
PUBLISHING DIRECTOR
Dan Savage
COMMERCIAL DIRECTOR
Nigel Hole
ASSOCIATE DIRECTOR
Malc Wheeler
BUSINESS DEVELOPMENT DIRECTOR
Terry Clark
MANAGING DIRECTOR
Brian Hill

Editorial address:
PO Box 99, Horncastle, Lincolnshire
LN9 6LZ
Visit our website:
www.classicmotorcycle.co.uk

General enquiries:
Tel 01507 529529, 24 hour answerphone
Email: help@classicmagazines.co.uk
Web: www.classicmagazines.co.uk

ARCHIVE ENQUIRIES
Jane Skayman
jskayman@mortons.co.uk 01507 529423

DISTRIBUTION
Comag, Tavistock Road, West Drayton, Middlesex UB7 7QE. Tel: 01895 433600

PRINTED BY
William Gibbons & Sons, Wolverhampton.

© Mortons Media Group Ltd. All rights reserved. No part of this publication may be reproduced or transmitted in any form or by any means, electronic or mechanical, including photocopying, recording, or any information storage retrieval system without prior permission in writing from the publisher.
ISSN No 978-1-906167-89-9

Contents

Triumph Bonneville
006 - 016

Barry Sheene
018 - 028

Cadwell Park
030 - 039

Vincent V-Twins
040 - 048

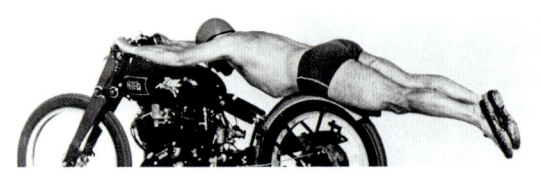

Jeff Smith
050 - 059

Norton Rotaries
060 - 069

Rockers
070 - 078

Velocette KTT
080 - 089

Brooklands
090 - 099

Geoff Duke
100 - 109

Scott Motorcycles
110 - 119

BSA Bantam
120 - 129

The beauty of the Bonneville; handling leads to fun times.

FLASH, BRASH & DANGEROUS TO KNOW

THE TRIUMPH BONNEVILLE

It may have been the antithesis of the staid pipe-smoking Brit machine but the Triumph Bonneville succeeded far beyond the dreams of its creators. It bestrode the world of motorcycling like a titan for more than a decade and just when its glory days seemed dead and gone it was born again for the modern age...

Is it Britain's most famous motorcycle? There are a couple more contenders to the throne, but one really has to admit that the Triumph Bonneville is the best known motorcycle ever to have been produced in Britain, which is ironic, considering that really it was instigated to sate the American market's demand for more power and could never really be considered as a 'quintessential' example of the British motorcycle industry in its boom years; surely a 'typical' Brit would be a sober, understated and rather conservative machine, most likely a single-cylinder machine, not a flash, brash and promisingly, alluringly dangerous to know US-tailored twin-cylinder offering.

Launched in late 1958 for the 1959 season, the Bonneville appeared with little fanfare. Indeed, on its launch (announced in the Press in October 1958) the first few words of the *Motor Cycling* preview ('Next Year's Triumphs') announced the discontinuation of the long-standing TR5 Trophy model before confirming the appearance of the 'Bonneville 120'. Specification was detailed later on, explaining that: "In recent years a comprehensive conversion kit has made possible increased use of the high-performance potential latent in the 500cc and 650cc engines – particularly the T110 – and it is the application of such parts which largely results in the existence now of a new '650' listed as the 'Bonneville 120'.

CLASSIC BRITISH LEGENDS 7

Minimal changes for 1970 – but it's what is reckoned by many to be the best-ever Bonnie.

"Cast-iron barrel and splay-inlet light alloy head carrying twin 1 1/16 in choke special Amal carburetters, with a remote rubber-mounted float-bowl, are standard: maximum performance derives from a Tiger 10 E3325 exhaust cam form in conjunction with an E3134 inlet camshaft. Standard valves and high-compression pistons (8.5:1) produce the 46bhp power output necessary for near 120mph road speeds."

But for the genesis of the Bonneville model, or at least its name, we must go back two years to the remarkable record breaking attempts by Johnny Allen. On September 6, 1956, Allen recorded a speed of 214mph on/in his Triumph twin powered, cigar-shaped motorcycle on the Bonneville Salt Flats, a record which although not officially ratified by the governing bodies due to some technical detail, gave Triumph and its ever-savvy chief Edward Turner the perfect name. Indeed, the legal wrangling and hoo-hah involved in the Allen case probably garnered more publicity than it would have done if everything had gone

Start of the lines – '59 'Tangerine Dream' this one with down turned bars and rearsets.

smoothly; it also added an element of 'renegade' to choosing that name for the new model.

The Bonneville was received enthusiastically for the most part, although it was quite quickly apparent that in reality the old single downtube Triumph frame and accompanying cycle parts – which were fine on a Speed Twin but admittedly almost 'at the limit' with even a Tiger 100 or Thunderbird, let alone a Tiger 110 – were now well-and-truly in the 'past it' category. Also unpopular in some circles was Triumph's choice of Tangerine; folklore claims it was due to the fact that poor Americans would buy old cars and paint them in garish colours and, somehow, this made the bright new Triumph look as if they too had been 'jazzed up'. Whatever, by midway through 1959, tangerine had gone, with blue – just like on so many Triumphs over the years – back in situ, in this case the shade being Royal Blue. The pearl grey remained.

The handling issues were addressed for 1960, with a new duplex frame instigated, though that itself had to be revised and strengthened during the year's run with an extra brace/tie added, while forks were improved too for better spring and damping action, plus cosmetic changes were instigated – the nacelle, which had been somewhat at odds with the model's intended usage, was dropped and separate headlight fitted, meaning the Bonnie looked more 'TR6-ish' – so much so, it was coded TR7 in the US. Colours remained as late 1960, Royal Blue and Pearl Grey.

There were minimal changes for 1961 – a change to Sky Blue and Silver and an 18in rear wheel among them – and again, 1962 saw little modification; chief visual

Above: Bonneville rider, left, on a 1959 version, looks across at the new 'unit' Triumphs.

Period maintenance on a 1964 Bonneville.

As good as the pre-units got – a super 1961 example.

difference was a two-tone dualseat, while the paint scheme remained the same in the UK, except that the oil tank went from silver to black. In the US, Flame (a metallic orange) replaced the Sky Blue.

After four years of listing, the Bonneville was now firmly established as the machine which sporting riders, particularly in America, bought or at least aspired to. Though there were some problems, often breakages caused by vibration and the sometimes dubious quality of proprietary electrical equipment, the Bonneville rose above it all – and fitted particularly into the American ethos of what motorcycling was all about; fun and speed, with a hint danger. Triumph was going from strength to strength in the States, with the colours, the speed, the style all slotting in well to the America ideal; problems were coming though, as Honda (and to a lesser extent the other Japanese makers) were doing in the smaller capacity classes what the big Triumphs were doing in the larger groups – i.e. dominating and giving the punter what was wanted. It'd all be alright, so long as Mr Honda decided to concentrate on 305cc and under…

›› continued on page 14

One for the racers – Thruxton Bonneville, displayed at the 1964 motorcycle show.

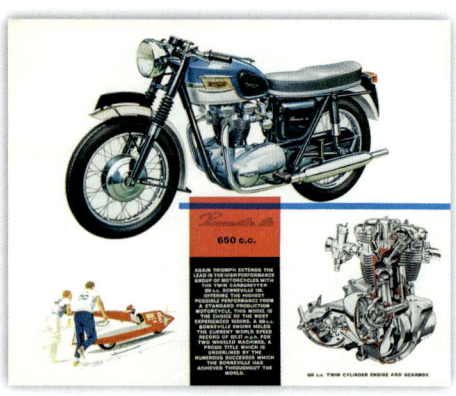

Compare and contrast the 1964 and 1965 brochure illustrations – little change really.

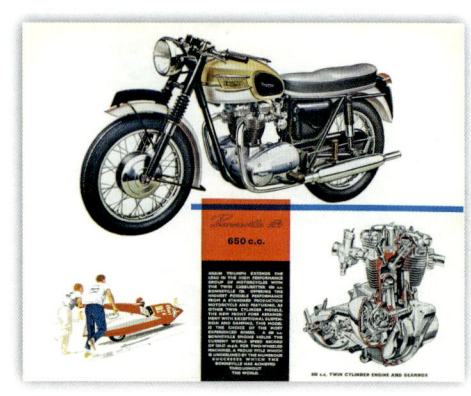

10 CLASSIC BRITISH LEGENDS

Above: This 1969 Bonnie is being exercised by Roger Beale.

Top right: *Motor Cycling's* Bernal Osbourne discusses the new unit Bonnie with Triumph stalwart Frank Baker.

Right: From 1971, first of the oil-in-frames.

Below: The fantastic, simple finish of the 1963 model exampled.

After four years of listing, the Bonneville was now firmly established as the machine which sporting riders, particularly in America, bought or at least aspired to.

Classic British Legends **11**

THE LUXURY SEAT

Designed for day long riding in great comfort. Softly upholstered in hard wearing materials. Ample size (23 ins. × 10 ins. × 5 ins. depth) and hinged for easy access to electrics mounted in a well protected area beneath the seat.

LARGE FOR SAFETY

Powerful large area tail/stop light giving maximum protection. Plated mounting bracket. Well spaced direction indicators.

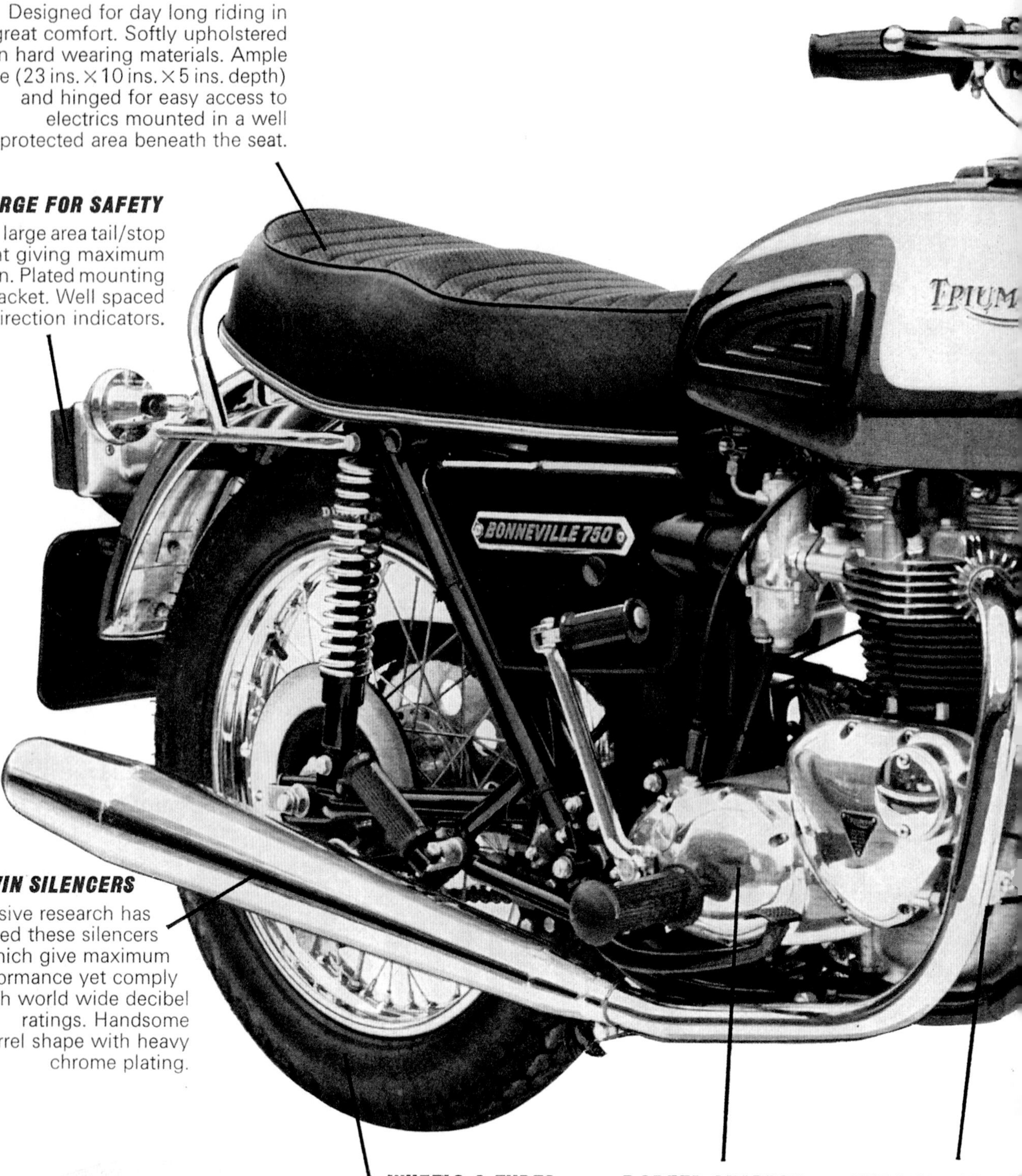

TWIN SILENCERS

Massive research has produced these silencers which give maximum performance yet comply with world wide decibel ratings. Handsome barrel shape with heavy chrome plating.

WHEELS & TYRES

Tyres are critical on a high performance motorcycle. The 'Bonnie' has Dunlop Gold Seal K70, renowned for adhesion under adverse conditions whilst ensuring handling of highest quality.

5 SPEED GEARBOX

The ultra robust Triumph gearbox built in unit with the engine. Five speeds, left foot operation. Heavy duty multi plate clutch.

THE 'BIG BONNIE'

A great engine, developed from its legendary 650 cc namesake. Redesig to cope with the e. power with new a stronger pistons, b oil pump, stiffer ro and so on. All addir to smooth effortles Triumph power.

For the rider who prefers the higher handlebar and small capacity fuel tank as supplied to USA, this specification is available in most markets.

BONNEVILLE and TIGER 750

By the mid-to-late 70s the Bonnie was back on track; this is 1976.

SUSPENSION
Race bred forks to give that certainty of handling under all conditions. Two way hydraulic damping, polished aluminium sliders, gaiters to keep out the dirt. Girling rear units adjustable for load.

FRONT DISC
Massive ten inch disc mounted on all alloy hub. A powerful and smooth acting brake hydraulically operated. Handlebar mounted master cylinder.

STOP PRESS — SPRING 1976
TIGER 750 TR7 reintroduced. The latest version of a long line of Triumph Twins combines the traditional virtues of thoroughbred handling with a power bonus from the bigger engine. Single carburettor design provides miserly fuel consumption of up to 75 m.p.g. with fuss free reliability.

CLASSIC BRITISH LEGENDS 13

UK spec, from 1980.

The T140ES, in police trim.

›› The first big upheaval in the Bonneville's life came in 1963 – unit construction was introduced (following from the earlier 3TA etc) while there was a new frame, too. Essentially, it was an all new motorcycle (though forks were as 1962) and marked the second stage of 'evolution' in the Bonneville's life. But like every other step or revision to come (possibly with the exception of the early oil-in-frames), the lineage was glaringly obvious.

Modifications continued to be made at a pace while there were new colours every year too; 1963 was the first 'all-one' colour, the striking Alaskan White (incidentally, the 350cc Tiger 90 was introduced and finished in the same colours year on year until 1968 – a 'Baby Bonnie' for those without the financial muscle to afford/run a Bonnie. A further acknowledgement that Triumph knew how the Bonnie proper was perceived).

In 1964 there were new forks and a

Another beauty – the 1969/70 model combined relatively light weight with a strong engine, decent brakes and fine handling.

14 CLASSIC BRITISH LEGENDS

gold-and-white, then Pacific Blue and Silver for 1965. From 1966, a split was made in that 'C' or 'TT' Bonnevilles – American market off-road sporting jobs – were offered in a different colour to the road going versions.

For many, the Bonneville reached its peak in 1968 – the year the twin leading shoe front brake was specified, while the forks were improved too, with two-way shuttle damping, plus there was a beefed up swinging arm as well. Amal Concentric carbs were now standard fitment (they came in during 1967). By now, the Bonneville could probably lay claim to be the most popular motorcycle in the world (a feat backed up by Production TT wins, starting with John Hartle's win in the inaugural 1967 event and Malcolm Uphill's famous 99.99mph race average, and 100mph lap, in the 1969 event) particularly in the US, where its star showed no signs of waning.

With hindsight, what Triumph should have offered with its 1969 Trident would have been a three-cylinder Bonneville, not gone off in a stylistic tangent – but that's hindsight for you.

The start of the Bonnie's decline came in 1971 – with what should have been a step forward. The oil-in-frame setup was introduced – and immediately drew criticism for a too lofty seat height. By 1973 two Bonnevilles were offered – the 650cc job and a 'bored out' 744cc version, the T140V, which featured a five-speed gearbox too.

During the 1970s and 80s Bonnevilles were increasingly viewed as antiquated and nothing more than an exercise in nostalgia – though a few special editions (1977's Jubilee and 1982's Royal Wedding, for example) caused a brief flurry of excitement, but little more.

Left: Les Harris, who built Bonnies under licence in the mid-to-late 1980s.

Bottom left: The Bonneville of the late 70s and early 80s was the ultimate development of a now aged design.

Below: High bars on a US spec, from the early 80s.

CLASSIC BRITISH LEGENDS 15

After Meriden's demise, Devon-based Les Harris built a few Bonnies under licence in the 1980s but that ended when 'new' (Hinckley) Triumph emerged. There was always going to be a new Bonneville – and it came, for the 2001 season. Borrowing styling cues and colours (the original 'new' one was in a 1968-aping paint scheme) from the past, it featured a 790cc, eight valve, chain driven double overhead cam engine. It was a hit straight away. Revisions, variations (the Scrambler, Thruxton, Bonneville America, Bonneville SE etc.) and special editions have followed, and the model continues to be popular.

Above: Special editions like the Silver Jubilee found favour.

Right: Bonneville Executive, with panniers, fairings and electric start.

Below: The early oil-in-frames didn't find favour – too high in the seat, cried the (not) buying public.

16 Classic British Legends

SPECIALISTS IN VETERAN, VINTAGE, CLASSIC AND THOROUGHBRED MOTORCYCLES

VERRALLS

A SELECTION OF MACHINES ARE ALWAYS AVAILABLE IN OUR SHOWROOMS

WE WELCOME QUALITY MACHINES IN PART EXCHANGE

WANTED - GOOD ORIGINAL VETERAN, VINTAGE, PRE WAR AND POST WAR CLASSICS. IF YOU HAVE SUCH A MACHINE AND YOU ARE INTERESTED IN SELLING, PLEASE WRITE OR PHONE AND SPEAK WITH IAN HATTON OR GORDON BUTTON

WE ARE OPEN TUESDAY TO FRIDAY 10am-5pm - SATURDAY 10am-4pm

THE OLD FORGE, QUICKS YARD, HIGH STREET, HANDCROSS, W. SUSSEX RH17 7BJ
Phone 01444 400678   Fax 01444 401111
Visit our website www.verralls.com

HANDCROSS IS 20 MINUTES DOWN THE M23 FROM THE M25

COCKNEY REBEL

BARRY SHEENE
Twice 500cc World Champion, Sportsman of the Year 1977, MBE, model, playboy, you name it, he lived it...

Motorcycle racers – or indeed any sportsman or woman from a 'minority' activity – have rarely 'crossed over' into the public's collective consciousness. But just as a policeman can still say; "Who do you think you are, Stirling Moss?' to a youth driving too fast and they'll (perhaps) know who's being referred to or at least understand the implication, so too does Barry Sheene remain the best known motorcycle racer Britain has ever produced. Sheene's combination of sheer speed, determination, rebellious streak and a chirpy, cheery demeanour, meant he was, in modern parlance, a marketing man's dream. The pace, the crashes, the outspokenness, the tenacity, the girls, the pop star pals, the talk shows, even the crash helmet design – it was all so right. Whether he was being tossed along the Daytona track surface like a rag doll, duking it out at high speed with Kenny Roberts in the British GP, posing in his pants for an advert or making merry with Henry Cooper in a Brut commercial, Sheene was everywhere.

Rounding the hairpin at Scarborough.

At the peak of his powers – the most famous motorcycle racer in the world.

With the 125cc Bultaco, at Snetterton, 1969.

On the Yamaha-powered Bultaco, Cadwell, 1970.

Barry Sheene was born September 11, 1950, living in a four bedroom flat in Holborn, London, WC1, which came as part of his father Frank's job as a maintenance engineer at the Royal College of surgeons. Frank had raced in the Isle of Man five times and in the 1960s, became friends with Francesco Bulto, head of Bultaco's racing concern. This led to Sheene Bultacos being a regular sight on the UK's racetracks.

So it was no shock Barry would be into his motorcycles. As a youngster, he spent most weekends in the race paddocks, while he had no interest in school. He'd also started smoking at nine…

It was inevitable he'd go racing and that happened, properly, in 1968, when he started competing on – naturally – Bultacos. By 1969 he was racing at national level and in 1970, his career clearly in the ascendency, he bought from Stuart Graham (for a whopping £2000) an ex-factory RT67 125cc disc-valve twin-cylinder Suzuki, which although four years old, was far and away superior to anything that the others racing on the British scene had access to – and Sheene had the talent to exploit it. Thing was, despite accusations that his was cheque book success, he still used the 125cc Bultaco to win the British Championship – he had his eye on a bigger prize with the Suzuki. On it, he made his GP debut in the season's last round, in Spain. He came second, behind home hero, Derbi's

The most important purchase of his fledgling career – the ex-Stuart Graham 125cc Suzuki.

Angel Nieto. The same meeting he also impressed on a 360cc Bultaco in the 500cc event, though it seized in the race.

He was intent on 125cc GP glory in 1971, though. To that end, he made an all out assault on the crown and if the type of points scoring system existed then as it does today, where all races count, he would have been world champ, but as it was then – when a rider dropped his worst five finishes from the 11 rounds – he ended up second. He still won three GPs though, while he often reflected himself that it was the best year of his career – he'd gone from a club racer to chasing international honours in two years. He was also on his way to becoming a fans' favourite – and star.

The next season, though, was an anticlimax, struggling to get the 250 and 350cc works Yamaha he'd landed on the pace and at season's end he was off back to Suzuki, with Seeley framed TR750 and TR500 for 1973. Soon, the career was well and truly back on track, winning both the domestic 500cc Shellsport Championship and the *MCN* Superbike series, and on the European stage, the FIM F750 Championship. For 1974, eyes were turned back on the 500cc GP class.

As a youngster, Sheene spent most weekends in the race paddocks.

Though there was an offer from MV Agusta, the dominant team for the last 15 years, what Sheene saw in Suzuki and its new 500cc square four persuaded him to stay. The RG500 offered a true 100bhp but it was, to say the least, 'scary' and kept breaking – but when it was going, boy was it fast… such was Sheene's confidence in it that despite some of the mishaps, it was alleged it was his belief and conviction in it which in the wake of the disappointing season (Barry could only manage sixth in the title chase) persuaded Suzuki not to ditch it and GP racing. At season's end, Sheene was off to Japan for an intensive testing rogramme.

The next year was when Sheene reckoned he'd gain superstardom – and he did. Thing was, he didn't do it as he expected – Barry's plan was to win the 500cc championship and achieve fame but what actually happened was he became a household name through a huge crash at Daytona… At 175mph, the tread stripped from his TR750's rear tyre and locked the back wheel. He was tossed like a rag doll down the track –

The TR500 provided some good rides in 1971.

many thought he was dead. He'd survived, but taken one hell of a beating – broken bones were left femur, right wrist, forearm, six ribs and collarbone plus kidney damage and massive skin loss. However, the dramatic footage of the crash made Barry Sheene a household name.

Injury forced him to miss the first two rounds of the 500cc GP chase, then he retired in the next two races. Round five was the Isle of Man TT where, like most of the top GP riders Sheene wasn't racing, then it was round six in Holland. There, with 150,000 fans looking on, Barry Sheene claimed his first GP victory – and he did it in style, passing Italian legend Giacomo Agostini on the last lap. Sheene only finished one other GP that season, in Sweden – but he won that one too.

The 1976 season was when it all came together – Barry Sheene seemingly won the 500cc GP championship at will, his works RG500 Suzuki a cut above the rest of the machines. Suzuki only made three full works bikes – and they all went to Sheene. The 'stock' available to buy RGs were good, but Barry's was better. Though the series was over 10 rounds, only six counted towards the championship; after seven rounds Barry had five wins and one second place, while

Above: Trying hard on the 'water buffalo' TR750 Suzuki, Silverstone, 1973.

Below: When it all started to come together; the RG500, here at Mallory.

Trying Mike Hailwood's TT winning Ducati for size in 1978.

Still pre-RG days – Suzuki GB racing manager Rex White with the 500cc twin, Sheene on the FR50 he'd bought his mum, Iris.

he hadn't contested the IoM TT. He then decided to miss the last three rounds, at road circuits, while also that season winning the British 500cc championship and the *MCN* Superbike crown. He was on top of the world.

There was an exact repeat the next year, while Barry Sheene – often with girlfriend Stephanie McLean in tow – was here, there and everywhere, loved by the tabloids, advertisers, small boys and grandmothers alike. By the dawn of 1978, he'd been awarded an MBE too, as well as the Sports Writers Association Sportsman of the Year for his 1977 exploits. What could possibly go wrong?

Californian Yamaha rider Kenny Roberts, that was what. While Sheene had enjoyed it pretty much his own way for the last two years, what with no other manufacturer's bikes being in the class of the RG and Barry getting the best of those, Roberts was an altogether different

>> continued on page 26

Below: At the peak of his powers – on the RG500, 1977.

1: The troublesome Pat Hennen provided some headaches in 1976.

2: Test of bravery through the Devil's Elbow, Mallory Park, 1978.

3: Early encounter with the nemesis – chasing Kenny Roberts in '77.

4: Donington Park, 1979, the Suzuki demonstrates its power.

5: Mallory Park, Yamaha TZ500, 1981.

6: Running his own team, with Akai backing.

Below: Lining up alongside Phil Read, on his customer RG, 1976.

Posing with girlfriend Stephanie McLean on the Ingersoll Watches stand – the GT500 was a competition prize.

Always make time for the fans...

Battling Roberts yet again, Donington, 1981.

»

proposition – and in 1978 it was he who bested Sheene, though a threat had developed from within the Suzuki camp in the form of American Pat Hennen, which evaporated when Hennen suffered career ending injuries at the Isle of Man TT. Some reckoned Hennen would have been 1978 500cc world champion, but it was Roberts who took it, from Sheene.

The next year, 1979, Sheene had slipped to third in the world reckonings – though there was the famous duel with Roberts at Silverstone in the British GP, which went the American's way – and for 1980 it was a switch to Yamaha in his own team. It didn't go great, though in 1981 he won the final race of the GP season in Sweden, his last ever GP win; but his star was on the wane.

There were flashes of brilliance, huge crashes (1982 at Silverstone) and what ultimately proved false dawns (back to Suzuki). His final GP season, 1984, provided some great performances, particularly if the weather was dodgy, and he called it a day at the end of the year, after negotiation to ride a works Cagiva stalled.

After moving to Australia in 1987, Sheene's profile lowered somewhat though he made various classic racing appearances, most notably at Goodwood, with a double win in the classic races at the 2002 British GP, on a Walmsley Manx Norton for which much of the crowd stayed behind. Soon after, it became known he had cancer – still, he raced at Goodwood that September, winning his final race with 80,000 looking on. He died March 20, 2003.

Right: Back on the RG500 and showing good form; Wayne Gardner, Keith Huewen and Wes Cooley, all on Honda triples, give chase.

Far right: Staying cheerful, by now on Yamaha.

Above: A 2001 appearance at Montlhery, France.

Below: Early Yamaha liaison in 1971; next season, works machines didn't work out as hoped.

MORTONS ARCHIVE
over a century of motorcycle memories

Recapture those once in a lifetime moments of motorcycling history with images from Mortons' extensive archive of preserved photos - all professionally reproduced in stunning quality and delivered to your door.

To order *action shots* or *nostalgic images* for private or commercial usage, contact Jane Skayman on the contact details below.

Tel: 0044 (0) 1507 529423
Email: jskayman@mortons.co.uk
www.mortonsarchive.com

Quality Assured

New WOLD ORDER

CADWELL PARK
Fondly nicknamed as the mini-Nürburgring, Cadwell Park has been the favourite circuit of many a rider and spectator alike. It still is... almost 80 years on from its first speed event.

Action from 1938 and (inset) Josh Brookes leaps The Mountain on the HM Plant Honda in 2010.

The most loved, most mythical, most spectacular racetrack in use in mainland Britain? Well, though perhaps Scarborough and Oulton Park may have claims to the title – Scarborough's albeit tenuous, as it's not a racetrack 'full time' – to many Cadwell Park and its awesome 'Mountain' has the crown firmly in its grasp.

Cadwell Park's story begins in 1926, when Mr Mansfield Wilkinson bought the land, approximately midway between Louth and Horncastle, so that he could enjoy shooting the local wildlife at weekends. Located on the cusp of the Lincolnshire Wolds, the natural gradients made the land unsuitable for farming, hence its use as a 'shooting' habitat. But Mansfield had a son, Charles, who liked motorbikes and it wasn't long before Wilkinson the younger was agitating at using a bit of the land for speed events; the first, organised under the auspices of Louth and District Motor Cycle Club (of which Charlie was secretary) was a hill climb held in 1933, in front of the Manor House, where Charlie Wilkinson lived later on and which served as the event offices and such.

Above: Poor quality but very early racing shot, taken at Barn Corner.

Left: Land owner Mansfield Wilkinson, who allowed his son to develop the circuit. Pictured in 1946.

By 1934, enthusiasm was sufficient that a race track was planned, on the old estate roads. It was over a rough three quarter mile circuit over what is not too far away from what enthusiasts would still recognise as the Woodland Circuit; basically, the start and finish was as it is now, with the track turning right to head up what's now the Mountain, then through Hall Bends, sharp right at the hairpin, before another right at Barn (then, where the old Barn actually stood) before back to the start-finish line, though those first few years, it was run in the opposite (anti-clockwise) direction, thus making the Mountain what must have been a scary, fast descent. Holes in the surface were filled with chalk and packed down with a road roller, though parts of the course remained grass.

The first race meeting was held on June 24, 1934, with a programme of five races – 250cc, 350cc, 500cc, handicap and sidecar. There was half price entry fees for Louth and District club members (2/6d, or 12.5p, as opposed to five shillings, 25p) while spectators had to lash out nine pence to gain admission – and plenty of them did – with another

From 1938, a Norton leads the field. Tommy Wood runs third.

three pence ('thrupence…') for a programme, printed by *Motor Cycling*.

The event proved popular with spectators and riders alike; soon, it was an established motorsport venue, with four races in the season's calendar. An early competition was for the Folbigg Trophy, awarded for the fastest time over eight laps. Among the early star performers (and winner of the trophy) was Alf Briggs, husband of 1940s and 50s off-road star Molly and later a major player in Honda's European operation, as well as being a personal friend of (and recipient of personally painted artworks by!) Soichiro Honda.

From the 1938 Good Friday meeting, the direction in which races were run had taken its current clockwise format, while the track had also been improved and

High speed action from 1947; Peter Goodman (Velo) leads, Alf Briggs (Triumph) is second, Les Dear (Velo) third.

Tommy Wood, one of the real Cadwell specialists. Machine is a KTT Velo, upwards of 10 years old at this postwar meeting.

Rickie Goodman gets his Norton somewhat crossed up at the Hairpin, in 1946.

CLASSIC BRITISH LEGENDS 33

Peter Davey, Vic Willoughby and Jacke Beeton try out the course alterations.

finished with either concrete or Tarmac; a vast improvement over the old dirt tracks. Every meeting attracting a vast crowd, while P Lansdale (normally on a 348cc Norton) had established himself as something of the man to beat, while Briggs was often his main challenger/vanquisher. At the August bank holiday meeting (incidentally, still Cadwell's biggest race meeting of the year, now for British SuperBikes) a BBC outside broadcast unit was present, with Graham Walker on hand to provide the commentary. To familiarise himself with the circuit, Walker (father of Murray and a former TT winner) did three laps on a borrowed Velocette.

There were more circuit improvements during 1939, while a newcomer established himself as something of a Cadwell star – a young man named Les Graham, for now aboard a works OK-Supreme JAP. At the May Whit Monday meeting, he swept all before him and won the still-going Folbigg Trophy to boot, too. Last of the prewar meetings was the August bank holiday event; youngster George Brown (later of Nero and Super Nero fame) was the day's star turn, on his 500cc HRD (Vincent), and despite a

Crowds look on in 1953.

Billie Nelson (Norton) leads like mounted trio Higgins, Greenfield and Brian Denehy into Hall Bends, 1961.

tumble at the hairpin in the woods, went on to win the Folbigg Trophy and set a new lap record – which remained for the duration of the war.

Britain's first postwar motorcycle road race meeting was held at Cadwell Park on Good Friday 1946. The place was packed, with an estimated 15,000 spectators turning up, to watch Maurice Cann (250cc Moto Guzzi) win the first race of the day. Tommy Wood won the 350cc race on his KTT, while George Brown, on the famous 'Speedway special' HRD/Vincent, took 500cc honours.

Major revisions took place in 1953 (just prior to which local hotshot Peter Davey set a new lap record), with the track length extended to a mile and a quarter – basically, what was added was the Coppice section, so up the hill, then a right back down what's effectively now Mansfield. Davey had become something of the man to beat; indeed, he'd taken part in that first postwar meeting, and was a circuit star. In front of over 40,000 at the August meeting, on the new track, he didn't disappoint winning both the 500cc and unlimited events on his Triumph-JAP; choosing to use the 'circuit special' rather than the Manx Nortons he had at his disposal. During the 1950s, Cadwell gradually grew and grew in popularity, with ever stronger grids assembled and the cream of Britain's road racing talent making the pilgrimage to Lincolnshire. But Wilkinson was savvy enough to recognise that he needed to maximise the venue's

Pip Harris over The Mountain, in 1954.

In 1952, Cyril Osbourne, MP for Louth, shows Mansfield Wilkinson a letter granting permission for course extensions. Chas Wilkinson looks in.

CLASSIC BRITISH LEGENDS 35

John and Cathy Tickle's Norton outfit heads Chris Vincent and Eric Bliss (BSA) and Rice/Rider (Triumph) in 1961.

Above: Chas Wilkinson displays his sartorial elegance in 1981, on a 500cc Norton.

Right: Phil Heath on his Norton in 1971, rounding Mansfield, during the Vincent OC Speed Trials.

See me, hear me... briefly... Mike Hailwood (Honda) streaks and shrieks into the lead, in 1966.

potential, so didn't limit it to just road racing; scrambling was booming and the pinnacle was reached when the 250cc British GP was held there, in 1964. Belgian's Joel Robert (CZ) was the winner, leading home a quartet of Brits (Dave Bickers, Malcolm Davis, Bryan Goss and Derek Rickman, the first three on Greeves, Rickman a Metisse) in front of a crowd of around 15,000.

Britain's first postwar motorcycle road race meeting was held at Cadwell Park on Good Friday 1946.

Other events included car races, motorcycle grass track and even greyhound racing…

But meanwhile there were more changes afoot for the circuit, particularly in 1961 when it was developed to what basically remains today. What had before been a right turn at Coppice Corner became a long, fast, left, leading into what was now named Charlie's, a right hander. This led onto the new, long Park Straight, at the end of which was the right handed Park Corner. This lead into Donington (later to be Chris Curve, after Chris Wilkinson, Charlie's son), through the right/left Gooseneck, down into Mansfield before heading towards the Mountain section. Though further bits have been added/amended, the circuit remains, largely, the same today.

In the 1960s and 70s, Cadwell continued to attract gargantuan crowds and superstar riders – the famous image of Giacomo Agostini leaping the MV over the Mountain remains an iconic one, while the likes of Mike Hailwood, Phil Read, Bill Ivy, John Cooper, Barry Sheene

Showing how it should be done over The Mountain – John Cooper, Norton, 1965.

Local man Derek Chatterton was a long-standing star of Cadwell. Here in 1966.

CLASSIC BRITISH LEGENDS 37

Above: From 1977. British Championship action at the hairpin; Malcolm Aldrick/Alan Gosling, 700cc Revett Yamaha.

Below: The 1964 British 250cc Motocross GP; this is Belgian Joel Robert, CZ.

and Mick Grant were regular visitors and winners too, though local hero Derek Chatterton, on his Chat-Yamaha, was a regular upsetter of the applecart. Also popular was stock car racing.

In 1987 Cadwell Park was sold by Charlie Wilkinson to Brands Hatch Leisure, the firm owned by the Foulston family. During the late 1980s and 90s, there were some improvements made – for example the club house was built – though the circuit remained largely as it was in the 1950s and 60s, with facilities gradually becoming somewhat dilapidated and behind the times. Still, though, the August BSB round continued to attract

huge crowds, while other meetings – including plenty of car events – were popular as well.

Cadwell Park was bought in 2004 by MotorSport Vision, the company run by former F1 driver Jonathan Palmer. Gradually, Cadwell has been improved; new toilet blocks, spectator facilities – including paths and steps – installed, the paddock area bettered, plus on track modifications for safety, including a new chicane meaning riders or drivers are slowed down before entering the Mountain section.

Cadwell's BSB round remains one of the most popular in the season's calendar, with 30,000 attracted to the circuit, to see some spectacular racing. Among recent highlight was an excellent performance by local Steve Plater, who won the 2003 Superbike race on his underpowered Honda SP1 twin, to the crowd's delight. Many spectators flock to the Mountain area to see what is undoubtedly one of the most spectacular sights in two-wheeled sport – a motorcycle launched over the top of The Mountain.

Above: Trevor Nation over The Mountain. The John Player Nortons did much to encourage crowds back to British tracks, Cadwell included.

Below: Geoff Barry (18), Derek Chatterton (22) and Stuart Jones (68) wait to get out on track, 1977. All are on Yamahas.

SNARLING BEASTS & BLACK SHADOWS

VINCENT V-TWINS

Few motorcycling icons can hold a candle to Vincent's incredible V-twins. A revelation when they first appeared, these classic British machines have stood the test of time and their high-performance engines are still held in the highest esteem worldwide...

Rollie Free in action – probably the most famous Vincent image of all.

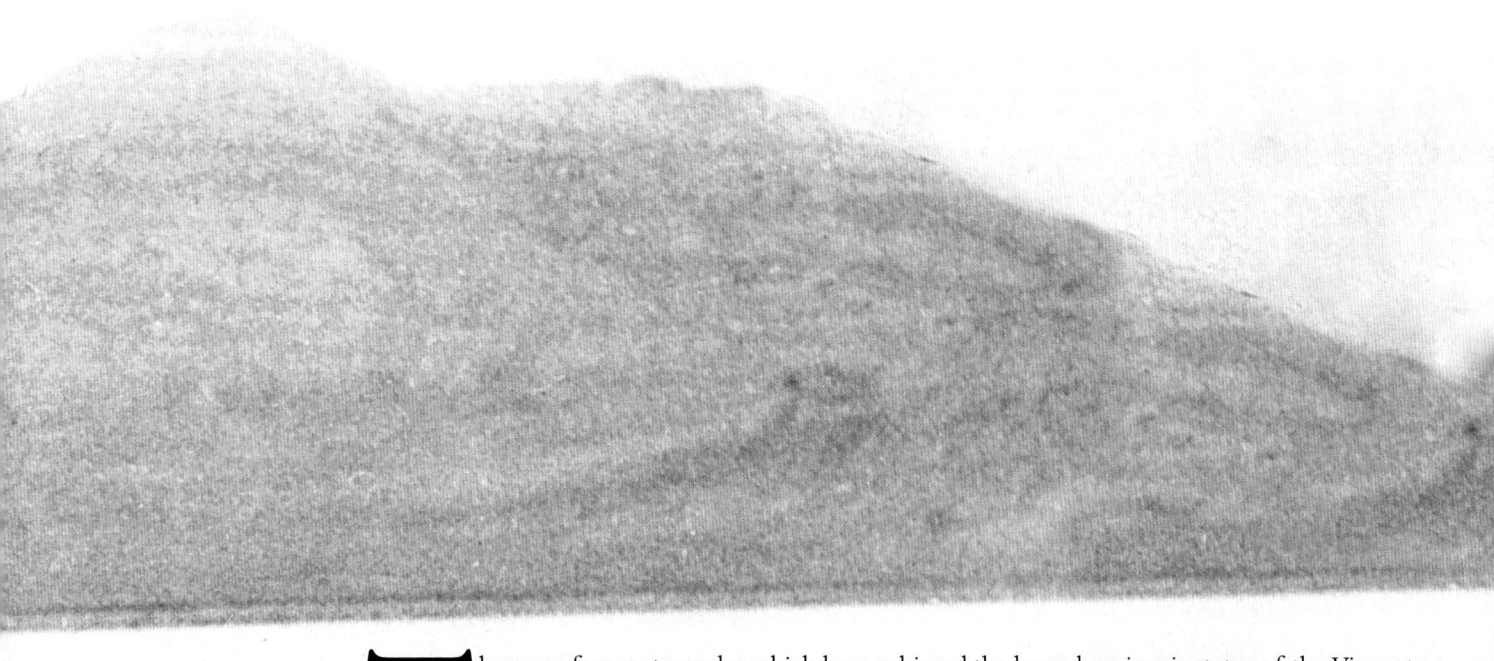

There are few motorcycles which have achieved the legendary, iconic status of the Vincent V-twin. Immortalised in song (Ian Dury cites them as a reason to be cheerful, while Richard Thompson dedicates a whole song, Vincent Black Lightning) and film (the choice of mount for the Thought Police in the film of George Orwell's 1984), even cartoonist Paul Sample relied on Vincent power for the motorcycle of his seminal 1970s cartoon character Ogri. Legendary 1970s-on automotive journalist LJK Setright also rhapsodised about them.

In the motorcycle world, the exploits of he-men such as George Brown (first with Gunga Din, then his Nero and Super Nero sprinters), American Rollie Free (he of the swimming trunks and lay-down posture), Kiwis Russell Wright and Bob Burns (record breakers), and London's Brian Chapman (Mighty Mouse and Super Mouse) and, today, the Australian Irving Vincent crew have kept the Vincent name in people's consciousness and maintained the marque's relevance.

An engine is set up to have its gears fitted, Stevenage, 1952.

CLASSIC BRITISH LEGENDS 41

Above: The first Series B twin made its debut appearance – Phil Vincent watches on.

Below: Series A Rapide, under test.

The man behind the motorcycle was Philip Vincent, a young Harrow and Cambridge educated engineering idealist, who had a vision of how he thought a motorcycle should be – and who stuck to his philosophy with a doggedness which ultimately was to prove his downfall. In 1928, he founded his company (Philip Vincent, or PCV, was just 20 at the time) with his Argentine-based wealthy father's backing, after buying the HRD trade name and soon was producing HRD-branded motorcycles, albeit in an incredibly limited number; also, for a company which was to produce arguably the most handsome motorcycling 'swans' of all time, those first offering were truly ugly ducklings. Relying on proprietary engines, gearboxes, front forks, hubs and such, what set the HRD (Vincent) apart was its rear springing; every Vincent machine ever made had rear suspension.

By the 1930s, PCV had grown tired of the somewhat disappointing performance of proprietary engines (the 1934 Senior TT was a particular nadir, when HRDs with JAP engines underperformed) and decided upon the need for a 'homemade' job. Brilliant Australian engineer Phil Irving was integral and, at the 1934 motorcycle show, the new 500cc single cylinder HRDs were unveiled – despite never having run, claims of 80mph for the cooking Meteor and 90mph for the Comet were confidently asserted.

And the new singles didn't disappoint, proving themselves entirely competent and indeed much better than much of the opposition. It is reputed (though unsubstantiated) that PCV was to claim many years later that the initial Comet was the best motorcycle his firm ever made. When one considers what came later, that means he really must have rated it.

Still, it wasn't enough for Vincent – he wanted more of everything. Legend goes that a 'coincidental' laying over of two drawings of single-cylinder Comet/Meteor engines led to the germination of an idea for a V-twin. Whatever, it soon became a reality and in

Top: Prototype Black Shadow – the machine is still extant.

Right: Series A twin, Clubman's day, Brooklands, 1939.

Of course, the Series A's speed made it popular for performance events early on – this from 1938.

CLASSIC BRITISH LEGENDS **43**

1: The fate of many twins – a Series B hitched to a large sidecar.

2: Competition sidecar twin, a Series C Rapide, used by one-legged (note the dual pedals) Harold Taylor in the 1948 ISDT.

3: Sectioned Series C Black Shadow.

1936, the first HRD Rapide was unveiled; and what a sensational machine it was.

For years, George Brough, with his rather pompously named Brough 'Superior' had lauded it as the maker of the fastest motorcycle in the world, the 'Rolls-Royce' of motorcycles, but now Vincent could challenge his claim. And while Brough's machine was undoubtedly exquisite, the HRD/Vincent offering was something else – chiefly because rather than just buying in all the best bits and assembling them, the HRD featured the firm's own engine and brakes.

The twin-cylinder HRD Rapide took on a legendary status, aided by fleeting (almost mystical) appearances in 'speed' events, such as when Stanley 'Ginger'

Record breaking at Montlhery in May 1952.

44 CLASSIC BRITISH LEGENDS

Wood turned up at 1938's Donington Parks August Bank Holiday meeting with a factory-prepared racing twin. Last away from the line, Ginger (a man not scared of a hairy-handling motorcycle; he'd raced, among others, New Imperial's 500cc V-twin) shattered the lap record before clutch trouble forced his retirement. But the sight and sound of him wrestling the 'Snarling Beast' lived long in the memory.

Indeed, clutch problems dogged the prewar HRD twins, with contemporary road tests complaining of clutch-slip above 100mph. With less than 80 twins produced, the Second World War put an end to production; during hostilities PCV's factory was involved in war work,

4: Ready for despatch to Argentina – first production 'B' Rapide, 1946.

5: Vision of the future – the all enclosed Series D.

6: Series D Black Shadow, cantered outside the works.

Below: Hub shells being machined in 1952.

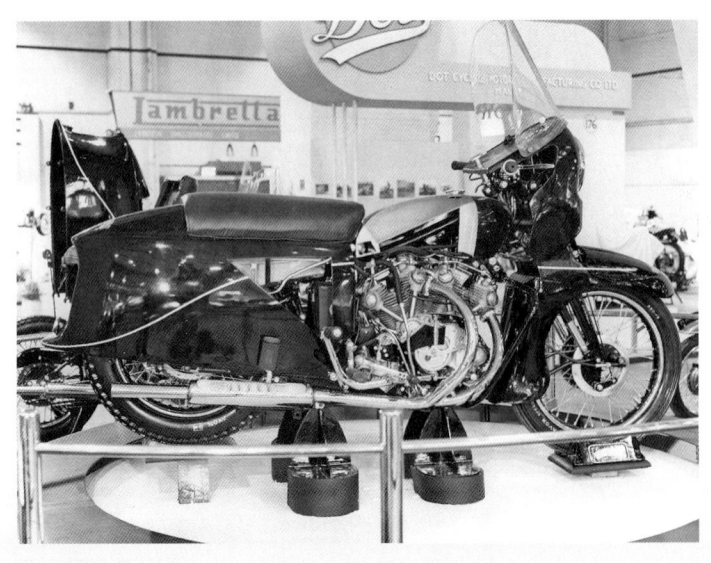

Sectioned D, showing what's under all those panels.

Touring Series C Rapide.

but that didn't stop plans being formulated for what was going to occur once the war was over. Chief among the problems which were going to tackled was the issue of that pesky underperforming bought-in transmission.

So it was no surprise that when the postwar version of the Rapide was unveiled it was substantially redesigned – and featured the firm's own gearbox/clutch. That wasn't the only difference to the prewar machine though; another radical step was the use of the oil-carrying spine frame, from which the engine/gearbox unit was hung and onto the back of which the rear suspension was mounted. If some accused the Series A of having rather the look of being 'cobbled together' (among its nicknames were the 'plumber's nightmare', due to the engine's oil pipes) the Series B looked every inch as if it had been designed 'as one' from the start.

Interestingly, and in a reversal of what happened 'prewar', this time a twin was effectively 'halved' to come up with a single (made in two road going versions, the Meteor and Comet, and racing Grey Flash), while an even 'hotter' version of the 110mph Rapide made its bow; the 125mph Black Shadow. With highly polished internals, an upped compression ratio, bigger carburettors and an all-black engine finish, it was something else. Suave and slightly sinister at the same time, the Black Shadow – which sounds like the name of a highwayman or Scarlett Pimpernell-esque dandy/vigilante, or DC comics creation –

A (fairly) typical mid-1950s scene – a B twin provides family transport.

Start of the 1950 Clubman's TT – Rapide riders are, left to right, Taylor, Lund, Carr and Davis.

was like nothing which had been seen before. The engine's performance (employing lessons learned by the Brown brothers, George and Cliff, and engineer Phil Irving in the tuning of 'Gunga Din', the factory hack/racer, a machine developed from a Rapide deemed too mechanically noisy to sell) and the motorcycle's braking capabilities were better than anything else available in the world and in excess of all but the very few top 'works' grand prix racing motorcycles in existence; and it would have given those a run for their money. And it was available for the man in the street to buy.

The B range – with HRD branding and Brampton girder forks – was replaced for 1949 by the C, which had Vincent's own 'Girdraulic' fork and soon Vincent appeared on the petrol tank too,

Right: Enclosure tipped up for access displaying the subframe and suspension differences from the Series C.

Below: Standard Series C Rapide, 1953 – note the black wheel rims, owing to chrome shortages.

CLASSIC BRITISH LEGENDS 47

First and last – well, nearly. The final Series D (Bruce Main-Smith in saddle) and the works' then own Series A.

Vincent popularity endured in the US – Ed La Belle attempts a Daytona record, in 1964.

George Brown, aboard his sprinter, Nero.

supposedly in response to alleged 'confusion' in the USA because of Harley-Davidson/H-D/HRD issues. The C is, to many, the ultimate incarnation of the Vincent V-twin, a machine which if anything is the most understated of all the Vincents. A Black Lightning V-twin had also appeared; a stripped and even-more tuned 'racing' Black Shadow, with 70bhp claimed, against the Shadow's 55 and the Rapide's 45. Most (a relative; very few were made) Lightnings were supplied for record breaking duties, though a few supposedly went out 'road equipped'.

The Series B looked every inch as if it had been designed 'as one' from the start.

The final Cs were dispatched in early 1955, by which time Vincent was heavily involved in producing its Black Knight/Prince models; basically, fully enclosed versions of the Rapide (Knight) and Black Shadow (Prince). However, various problems meant that 'naked' variants of the models were made, with the old names revived too, in the form of the Series D Rapide and Black Shadow. These, though, had lost the oil carrying frame, with oil now carried beneath the seat, had a different rear subframe complete with ugly seat, smaller wheels, and even the 5in speedo that so enhanced the Black Shadow had gone. Even the naked Ds looked portly, a poor relation to the beautifully proportioned machines which had gone before. The last V-twin Vincent, a Black Prince, was made in December 1955.

It wasn't the end of the Vincent V-twin. It was to be nearly 15 years before another motorcycle entered production which was genuinely faster than a Vincent V-twin, so the models remained immensely popular. The owners club continued to thrive, while Vincent engines were still the power unit of choice for many record breakers, drag racers and hill climbers, the likes of George Brown, Ian Ashwell (Satan), Charlie Rous (MotoVin) and Maurice Brierley (Methaman) among them.

These days, it is possible to build a Vincent brand-new from the parts which are available via the Owners Club; indeed, the club did that a year or two back, to showcase its scheme.

1962 – FIFTY YEARS OF THE 59 CLUB – 2012

MAGAZINE OF THE FIFTY-NINE CLUB

59 LINK — May 1965 — Price 1/-

Father Bill
Bronx jacket by Lewis Leathers
www.lewisleathers.com

Lewis Leathers congratulates the 59 Club on the magnificent achievement of their 50th anniversary. Best wishes for continued success and Safe Riding always.

Lewis Leathers

"One man's trash is another man's treasure..."

Old Bike Mart

Old Bike Mart is known and loved worldwide as 'the autojumble in your armchair' and 'the restorer's Bible'. Old Bike Mart is a newspaper dedicated to the world of vintage, classic and post classic motorcycling. Subscribe today for only £16. Direct from Mortons Media Group Ltd.

Call 01507 529529 or visit www.oldbikemart.co.uk

Quality Assured

Want to keep that authentic look but not pay over the odds?

All our Aluminium plates are produced using handmade, traditional methods using original dies, traditional 1950's presses & stoving finishes. We can even produce custom made shapes replicating original templates!

Interested? Call us now on 0114 273 1151
or visit our website: www.jepsonandco.com

JEPSON & CO LTD
THE ORIGINAL NUMBERPLATE
Est. 1894

In action at Halstead, in June 1968.

SIMPLY the BEST

JEFF SMITH MBE
Twice FIM 500cc Motocross World Champion, twice British Trials Champion, multi British Experts trials wins, a Scottish Six Days Trials win and eight ISDT Gold medals… and there's more…

The greatest scrambles (or motocross as it became) rider Britain has ever produced? There's no argument really – it has to be Jeffrey Vincent Smith, the Colne, Lancashire, born rider, synonymous with BSAs, who from 1953 until 1971 was right at the top of the trials and then scrambling trees. He won 17 major titles for BSA, including the 500cc world motocross crown in 1964 and 1965.

What's often overlooked is the fact Smith was also a mighty fine trials rider, winning every major British trial and title too, in 1955 triumphing in the Scottish Six Days and the British Experts, while the previous year he'd won his second successive ACU Star, also known as the British Championship.

Smith had started relatively young. He had his first motorcycle, a 1929 Triumph, aged 13, in 1947. By then, the Smith family had left Lancashire for Birmingham, though young Jeff (he shared his father's name and initials) always retained his Lancs brogue and indeed bore the county's Red Rose on his crash helmet throughout his career. Though he had his Triumph, petrol was in short supply, so tinkering was the order of the day – but that stood him in good stead anyway. By 15, he'd won his first trial, an all off-road closed to club event.

Pictured in the world championship year of 1965.

CLASSIC BRITISH LEGENDS 51

Pressing on aboard the C15, 1959.

At 16 his father (himself a keen competitor) bought Jeff a BSA Bantam, meaning he could compete in open-to-centre trials, as he was now road legal. Passing his motorcycle test proved easier said than done though – despite his precocious talents, it took him three attempts, though that was mainly due to treating the test like a time trial, trying to do it in the shortest possible time…

By 1951, Jeff Senior had realised that his boy was a bit special, so handed over his 500T Norton to the 17-year-old, who meanwhile had started a five-year apprenticeship at BSA on the first day of

Nose heavy landing at the 1954 Experts Grand National, on the Goldie.

During the 1955 Austrian Alpine Trial – note the aviated front wheel.

52 CLASSIC BRITISH LEGENDS

Whoa there! The works rigid BSA gets a bit lively in December 1953.

Classic British Legends 53

Mud covered in France, 1960 Motocross Des Nations.

The 1960 Beenham Jackpot scramble.

Pushing on in 1960, in Europe.

1951. Soon, the young man was in the trials winners' circle, securing his first national victory in the Shropshire Traders Cup Trial which qualified him for the British Experts Trial – he duly ended up an astounding fourth place, tying with Bill Nicholson, the experienced and brilliant Northern Irishman. Indeed, it took a big effort by Nicholson in the special test to best the youngster, after they'd tied on marks lost. He also claimed a Gold Medal in the ISDT. His efforts didn't go unnoticed – Norton drafted him into their works squad for 1952, meaning he was in an unusual position, riding a works Norton at the weekend, then going to work at BSA on Monday… order was restored when, in 1953, he was named part of the BSA squad.

On BSA, he was soon a regular winner, meaning that in 1953 he won the ACU Star. He was just 19. Next year, 1954, he was even more successful, taking another ACU Star as well as another ISDT Gold.

In 1960, Jeff Smith started his true domination of scrambling, especially at domestic level.

But Jeff Smith had decided it was in scrambling where his future lay. He was as spectacularly good at that as he had been at trials too – by the end of 1955 he'd earned his first ACU Star in that field. Machines he campaigned were BSA Gold Stars; indeed, on the Goldies in his first season (1954) he was fourth in the chase for the Star, as well as third in the European Championship.

During the latter half of the 1950s he went from strength to strength; there were notable wins in the British Motocross GP (1955, 1957 and 1959), back to back British championships (1955 and 1956), he was a starring member of several victorious British Motocross Des Nations teams (in 1955, 1956 and 1957 he was the British team's best scorer, as they won year on year) while he was also second, on a C15, in the 1959 250cc Motocross GP.

The 500cc motocross world championship started in 1957, held over eight rounds. Jeff Smith was among the favourites but didn't enjoy the best of world title seasons, British GP and Motocross Des Nations aside, and had to settle for fourth place; Bill Nilsson, abandoned by BSA and now AJS

The 1956 St David's Trial.

mounted, though AMC had also withdrawn its support so his 7R-based special was tagged a Crescent, was the victor. The British Championship was cancelled, owing to the Suez Crisis.

In 1958 and 1959, Smith was sixth in the 500cc 'worlds' while he was still competing in trials too – there was a hat-trick of wins in The Perce Simon Memorial Trial, as well as numerous other awards too.

In 1960, Jeff Smith started his true domination of scrambling, especially at domestic level. He was the 500cc champion – it was the start of a six-year winning sequence, an unprecedented and surely never to be equalled feat. In the 250cc European Championship, Smith – on the new 250cc C15 – took the fight to the two-strokes, eventually finishing runner-up to the 'Coddenham Flyer'

Motocross Des Nations team – the ACU's Eddie Davidson, team manager Haines, then Les Archer, John Burton, Don Rickman, Dave Curtis and Jeff Smith.

Comparing notes with journalist Peter Fraser in 1963.

CLASSIC BRITISH LEGENDS 55

Jeff Smith, Dave Bickers and Joel Robert compare notes.

Textbook style aboard the Goldie, 1960.

Dave Bickers, on his Greeves. Next year, Smith was third in the 250cc class again, while in 1962 – with the series now granted world status – he was runner-up again, this time to Sweden's Torsten Hallman. Meanwhile, of course, he was still winning the British 500cc championship – though the faithful old Goldie was becoming rather long in the tooth while BSA had actually ceased making it.

After three years of tying to (unsuccessfully) claim the 250cc world title, BSA decided to switch its attentions to the 500cc class – with a specially enlarged version of the old 250. The 350cc B40 was taken as the basis, with capacity stretched to 420cc. Smith was to spearhead the assault, supported by Arthur Lampkin, while John Burton was also employed, aboard a Gold Star. BSA

Training with Olympic hurder Maurice Herriot, in the grounds of Small Heath.

didn't quite manage the win it was hoping for, but the new model showed real speed and potential, allowing Smith – now aged 30 – to finish third in the chase, just two points down on runner-up Sten Lundin, trailing title winner Rolf Tiblin. Lampkin was fifth – with a winter of development, surely the BSA would come good.

By now, Smith himself had recognised that as well as his motorcycle being in fine tune, he needed to be too. To that end, he trained harder and more often than anyone – while the new BSA was

Above: During the 1952 Scottish Six Days Trial, on the 500T Norton.

Below: Trials Bantam outing in the 1970 Northern Experts.

CLASSIC BRITISH LEGENDS 57

Main: The winner's spoils, a familiar feeling in 1965.

Right: At Farleigh Castle, 1967.

58 CLASSIC BRITISH LEGENDS

High flying in 1968.

Last season on the works BSA – Newbury in 1971.

being further developed and honed in readiness for the 1964 title challenge, Smith was doing similar to himself. BSA employee and Olympic hurdler Maurice Herriot (who won a silver at the 1964 Tokyo games) devised an incredibly tough fitness regime for Smith, which involved running up 45 degree hills something like 20 times – and this was all done in their lunch hour. Apparently, Smith would be left staggering and dazed at the punishment his body was enduring.

But it all paid off – there was second place finishes in the first four rounds behind Tiblin, before Smith won in Italy – and Tiblin failed to finish. He won again overall in Russia, then Luxembourg, a second in West Germany, a win in East Germany, which set it all up for the final round in Spain – where the title would be decided. Smith won both legs. The title was his.

He dominated the world series the next year, with the Victor now at 441cc, winning six events by July and keeping his crown. However, his period of domination was coming to an end – there was a last British crown in 1967 and a 250cc triumph in the 250cc BBC Grandstand Trophy and, having been made an MBE in 1970, he retired when BSA's competition shop closed in 1971. Next stop was a move across the Atlantic, where he was employed by Can-Am, helping develop the firm's 250cc racers, to such an extent that they filled the first three places in the prestigious AMA Championship. Smith settled in Wisconsin, where he continues to reside, though he makes regular trips across the water to classic events, plus an annual pilgrimage to the Irish National Rally – where he pilots a sidecar outfit provided by his old sparring partner Dave Bickers.

Trying really hard, in 1966.

During the 1965 500cc British GP.

CLASSIC BRITISH LEGENDS 59

The winning combination – Steve Hislop poses with the Norton on which he won the 1992 Senior TT.

The COOLEST ROTARY CLUB...

ROTARY NORTON

By the turn of the 1980s, it seemed like the once proud Norton name was lost and gone forever, the last Commandos having been built in 1978. But 1979 was to herald the arrival of Norton's first rotary engine, which had a somewhat chequered career...

During the 1970s some feasibility studies had been carried out, initially at BSA (part of the Norton group post 1973) into the possibility of using the Wankel rotary engine concept in a motorcycle. The first rotary engined machines were built in 1979, by Norton Motors (1978) Ltd, and a MkII version was built during 1981. Though beset by problems, created by funding issues and subsequent delays, the Interpol 2 was finally ready to be supplied to police forces and during 1983, over 130 were supplied, with additional machines sold to the army, navy and RAF, plus a quantity to the RAC too. The numbers weren't huge but it was a start – new Nortons were on the road.

There was a public clamour for a version to be made available to the public – and in 1987 that wish was granted, with the launch of the traditionally styled Classic model. By now, Norton had been taken over once more, this time by an investment group headed by Canadian Phillippe Le Roux. The Classic 'run' was limited to 100 (though 105 were made) – and all sold quickly.

It could've been a contender – high price made the F1 only available to the wealthy few.

CLASSIC BRITISH LEGENDS **61**

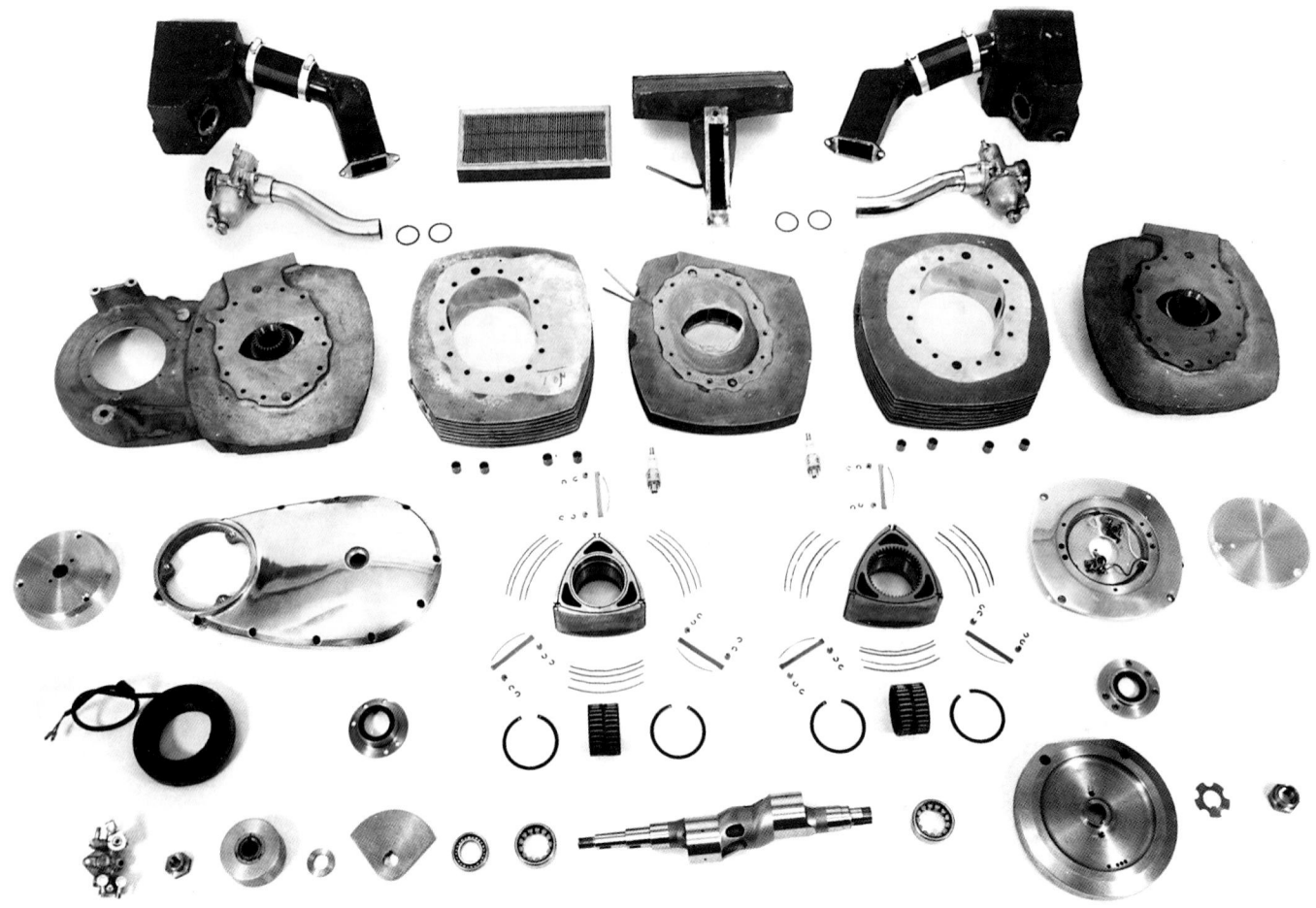

The start of something; the NVT prototype Wankel engine stripped bare.

Around the same time, a young development engineer, Brian Crighton, oversaw the debut of a rotary-powered racer he'd been working on, codenamed the RC588 and 'green lighted' by new Norton chief Phillippe Le Roux, who had recruited Crighton back into the Norton fold, after he'd left and been working in the aero industry. Ridden initially by factory road tester Malcolm Heath, it was immediately apparent there was potential there, as Heath raced it to third place in its debut at Darley Moor. That original bike was a true 'bitsa' using all sorts of components, sourced from various places – the frame was by Spondon, Kayaba forks came from an RG500 Suzuki, wheels (17in) were from Dymag and an Öhlins rear shock. The two carburettors were 34mm Amal Concentrics (the road bikes used SUs) while the gearbox was 'stock' Interpol 2, though the clutch was 'beefed up.'

But it was the engine which was the heart of the matter. The initial bike – like the roadsters – was air-cooled, but a crucial difference was that it used induction air to cool the rotors. Crighton's cleverly devised system – essentially providing an airway through the rotors – cured one of the problems which had bugged the police issue machines particularly – overheating.

The handsome and successful Police issue Commander.

An Interpol is inspected at the BMF show.

62 CLASSIC BRITISH LEGENDS

There were some problems with the officiating bodies of racing, something which was to continue to 'bother' the racers throughout. Basically, while the ACU allowed the rotary to run as 588cc, the FIM said it was 1176cc – arrived at by dint of taking the capacity of a combustion chamber times the number of rotors and doubling it, as they would for a forced induction engine, which the rotary wasn't. Crighton, meanwhile, insisted capacity was arrived at by taking the capacity of a single chamber and multiplying it by the number of rotors, giving 588cc.

Top: Classic was what fans were clamouring for; the air-cooled rotary became an instant favourite.

Bottom: Engines under assembly at Shenstone.

Top left: The red, blue and silver early air-cooled racer.

Top right: Spray again, at Brands, Good Friday 1990; he crashed just after this picture, remounting to come fifth.

Below: Steve Spray was another who enjoyed lots of early success on the Rotary.

For 1988, there was a proper race team, consisting briefly of Heath, Trevor Nation and Simon Buckmaster, with the trio campaigning red, silver and blue air-cooled rotaries. Buckmaster didn't last long either and his place was taken by highly rated youngster Steve Spray who took to the machine immediately; Spray's victories in a Powerbike race and the final round of the 1988 Formula One series brought Norton to prominence and in an act of neat symmetry, a deal was done so that Nortons would, once again, be backed by the John Player cigarette brand, just as they had in the early 1970s. Only difference now was John Player's corporate colours were black and gold – so that would be the colours for the rotary racers.

In 1989, the works racing team consisted of Steve Spray and Trevor Nation, on the stunning black, silver and

64 CLASSIC BRITISH LEGENDS

Sign of the future, in the shape of an early Rotary Roadster – the forerunner to the production Classic.

Machines in various stages of assembly – it all seemed to be going so well...

gold racers. The reappearance of Nortons, and their winning performance, saw crowds flock back to the race tracks of Britain. Spray in particular excelled, winning the British F1 and Supercup championships. However, all was not well behind the scenes and when Barry Symonds became race team manager, it wasn't long before Crighton found his position untenable and he moved on, setting up the Roton team. In 1990 Trevor Nation had excelled, while Spray had struggled; Spray left Norton and went to Roton, while Ron Haslam joined the JPS race effort alongside Nation.

The reappearance of Nortons, and their winning performance, saw crowds flock back to the race tracks of Britain.

While there was success on the race tracks, there had been sporadic road models too. The Commander followed the Interpol 2 for the police and a civilian version was launched in 1988. Though

TREVOR NATION
JPS NORTON

Nation's name was to become synonymous with Rotary race joy.

Mark Farmer keeps the Roton ahead of Haslam.

the Commander was worthy enough, with the race success, what fans were clamouring for was a road going 'race rep'. That came, of sorts, with the 1989 F1, though its performance was disappointing to anyone who expected a full-on replica of the racer with lights.

Nobody, though, could argue with its exclusivity or with its sunning looks.

Backed up with a memorable advertising campaign ('Bitch'/'Son of Bitch' with pictures of the racer and the new roadster) the F1s were phenomenally expensive and when it came to it, the performance wasn't really that much better (or any…) than say Honda's new CBR600; the Norton cost £12,700, and for that you could buy three of the Hondas. In a bizarre piece of marketing, when it didn't sell Norton put the price up further… But exclusivity meant that it did find some buyers, with 210 sold between 1990 and 1992.

Meanwhile, the racers continued to run at the front of British championships. Mark Farmer replaced Spray at Roton, while Robert Dunlop joined Haslam at

The all-conquering team; 'architect' Brian Crighton stands central.

66 Classic British Legends

Ron Haslam, in action during 1991.

First year with JPS sponsorship – the early air-cooled racer.

JPS – but the big news was in the Isle of Man where in the 1992 Senior TT, Steve Hislop raced an all-white Norton (actually, the same bike Haslam rode, with special dispensation, in the 500cc British GP) to a sensational win in one of the most memorable races in TT history. During an epic battle with Carl Fogarty on the Loctite Yamaha OW01, the pair lapped at ridiculous speed – on the pace they'd managed the year before, aboard Honda's RVF750 V-fours, the then-most-expensive, sophisticated four-stroke racers in the world. Despite the Nortons/Rotons track success, the money was running out and the factory team disbanded, with the Roton team taking over the 'factory' mantle, becoming Crighton Norton. Riders like Jim Moodie, Phil Borley and Ian Simpson enjoyed success, it culminating in Simpson winning the British championship on a Duckhams backed bike, in a team run by Colin Seeley. At season's end, though, the rotary was outlawed as British Championship rules were changed and Seeley, Simpson et al took up the Honda effort. And that seemed to be that, for then at least.

Meanwhile, with road bikes, an F1

Veteran racing journalist Ray Knight tests an early incarnation of the racer.

CLASSIC BRITISH LEGENDS

Nation pushing hard...

Sport had been launched too – and this seemed a lot more like it, ditching as it did the F1's 'jelly mould' styling in favour of something which more closely aped the racers. Built in strictly limited numbers (less than 40) it added to the small numbers of road going rotary Nortons built over the years, with figures reckoned on being 360 Interpol 2s, 300 Commanders and 105 Classics.

An interesting potential development was the F1R, supposedly a 'racer' which was going to revolutionise privateer participation, enabling them to buy their own rotaries and 'have a go.' Unfortunately, like so many Norton rotary 'possibilities' it amounted to nothing.

There was one final, last hurrah for the rotary Nortons, when, after the marque's acquisition by Stuart Garner and after some record breaking efforts in America, a rotary racer appeared in practice for the 2009 TT races. Alas, it wasn't to be the success it had hoped, with Michael Dunlop (son of Robert) failing to qualify after a host of problems. When Norton appeared for the 2012 TT, the racer now featured a V-four Aprilia motor, it seeming that the Rotary's racing days were, finally, done.

Out on track – Trevor Nation on board the evocative racer.

68 CLASSIC BRITISH LEGENDS

Following the British GP of 1992 – Ron Haslam enjoys a well-earned drink.

L for LEATHER

ROCKERS

Infamous through the hype of the local Press, Rockers ruled the highways in the 1960s with their black leather jackets, cafe racer style Triumphs – other models were available – and their rebellious lifestyle... is it time for a comeback?

During the early 1960s there were two primary motorcycling youth movements – 'mods' and 'rockers.' As much an anything, they – and their supposed live fast, die young mentality and depraved lifestyles – were inventions of the Press, but there were, like every press invention, elements of truth in it all. Mods we'll leave for another time, turning our focus to Rockers. So, what was it all about? Well, it was motorcycles, mates, music, girls, grease, cafes and coffees, Gold Stars and Bonnies, Eddie Cochran and 'Sweet' Gene Vincent, Elvis Presley and Jerry Lee Lewis. Mentality was one of rebellion, (it always brings to mind the Marlon Brando, Triumph Thunderbird-riding character Johnny in *The Wild One*; "What is it you're against?" "Whadya got?") and excitement, an escape from the often grey drudgery of 1950s/60s Britain.

Brighton front, 1965.

CLASSIC BRITISH LEGENDS **71**

It was all about motorcycles, mates, music, grease and girls...

The 'Rocker Dream' – pretty girl, Goldie engine in a Manx Norton rolling chassis...

Motorcycles were of course the central thing to the Rocker cult. Unlike Teddy Boys, with their elaborately coiffeured hair and drape suits, Rockers were more functional – because the bikes were the key. Though nowadays everyone assumes it was all Gold Stars, and while that may have been what many aspired too, actually Triumph twins were the much more usual rocker's machine of choice, and they weren't usually bang-up-to-date ones either.

Other regular fare, if you study the pictures, were the much more basic and simple offerings – hopped up plunger-framed B31 Beesas, racerised rigid G3L Matchies, Tiger Cubs with leopard print seat covers... sure, a few of the flash

And the more likely reality. Two-up, aboard a tired out Beesa C12...

He's got the look, 1960.

72 CLASSIC BRITISH LEGENDS

We two young tearaways... picking up Continental GT Royal Enfields, in 1965.

'arries had Bonnies and Goldies, but most made do with an old Thunderbird, its headlamp nacelle chucked in a bin, the handlebars turned upside down and rearset footrests home fabricated, with the silencers replaced by megaphones too.

The Rocker movement could be traced back to the mid-1950s, with most reckoning on 1956 as the year it all really got into its swing, thanks largely to the emergence of Rock and Roll which, coupled with Teddy Boy fashion from a little while before, came together to create what we now know as Rockers today. Bill Haley's *Rock Around the Clock* was the soundtrack to that budding emergence, while sensationalist media picked up on the new rock and roll scene reporting riotous behaviour, obviously caused by the music – not the fact that youngsters in Britain had, since time begun, simply gone from childhood to adulthood and had nothing in between – now with an emerging media and

Unwelcome attention in 1961. BSA is a Super Rocket.

CLASSIC BRITISH LEGENDS

Maintenance...

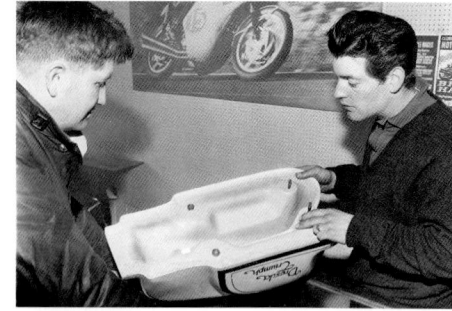

Dave Degens shows off a glass fibre petrol tank.

Well turned-out 'big' Royal Enfield twin.

exposure to other countries through various means including music, films and TV, through increased personal freedom by various modes of transport a new thing was happening, a new 'thing' was being created – the teenager.

Jimmy Dean's character Jim Stark in *Rebel Without a Cause* was their 'model' (a propensity for flick knives was also prevalent in period, possibly also influenced by the knife-fight scene in the film) with his surliness, his rebellion – and his downright coolness. The grown ups just didn't get it!

So, on one hand there were models to base one's self on, and on the other there was a soundtrack to go along with it. All that was needed now was a bit of tweaking, the claiming of an 'outfit' and, voilla, a cult is created.

After the outfit had been identified (black leather jacket, as modelled by Brando in *The Wild One*, though of course that hadn't been seen in the UK yet – made in 1953, it was banned until 1967 – black leather or denim jeans, black boots with sock tops rolled over,

Tool of choice. Triton receives attention.

The end is nigh; a Rocker looks over a Starfire BSA in 1968.

AJS Model 16CSR.

74 CLASSIC BRITISH LEGENDS

gloves – not gauntlets – and perhaps a crash helmet…) transport was the next issue to get to grips with.

Triumph twins were an obvious choice for four of the simplest reasons – they were plentiful, they were relatively cheap, they were fast… and they looked darned good. Though later it was the Bonneville which became the one people assumed all rockers had, a 'Ton ten' (Tiger 110) was a more likely machine, though the cooking Thunderbird was popular too. Triumphs were always that little bit quicker than their direct BSA equivalent – a T-bird would and will see off a stock A10… – while Nortons were a bit more exclusive and expensive, Matchless/AJS a tad staid (and more costly) and the likes of Velocette Venoms more likely to be 'enthusiast' owned than by tearaways, so the Triumph reigned supreme.

Sensationalist Press reporting did more to further the Rocker cause and profile than anything else; despite the intention being to have the opposite effect. While articles offered centred around the Ace Cafe – the spiritual home

Adding another badge to the black leather, in 1965.

Who's that girl? Miss P Maitland, in Norfolk, 1965.

Covering up.

Girls and boys, with 'ton up vicar', the Rev Bill Shergold.

of the Rocker – and were aimed at demonising and dissuading but as we all now know, if you tell teenagers to do something, their natural predilection is to do the opposite… It's even reckoned that one of the great Rocker 'trademarks', the racing over the duration of a record, was perhaps invented (or at the very least 'publicised' into wider consciousness) by one of the articles, which featured headlines such as 'Suicide club.' Balanced, then…

Though standard Triumph and Beesas were the hardcore of the early years of the Rocker movement, by the 1960s something else was in germination – the special building boom. In particular, the Triton. While in the late 1950s the Gold Star was the machine Rockers aspired to, rather than owned, the Triton was a much more common phenomenon.

The formula was simple – take a Norton frame and running gear (if you were lucky, it would be a Manx, discarded by the Formula 3 car racing fraternity in the 1950s and sold on for a song, but more likely a 350cc Model 50…) and

Off for a ride.

76 CLASSIC BRITISH LEGENDS

The smile – and the wording – says it all.

shoehorn into that a 650cc Triumph engine (again, if you were lucky, that would be a tuned Tiger 110 or Bonnie, with its twin carb head, but again, more likely, a Thunderbird…). Add to the mixture – not necessary if you'd started with a Manx – clip on bars, rear set footrests, rear swept exhausts, Goldie silencers, a great big alloy tank and some other polished bits and pieces, then what you had was the Rocker of the 1960s' motorcycle of choice. What was ended up with, was a machine which offered race-bred handling and a motor which had plenty of power – it was as quick as anything on the road. However, if one was particularly lucky – or well-heeled – then by the mid 1960s another machine had replaced the Triton as top of the pile – the Norvin. Basically, follow all of that detailed above but rather than a Triumph engine, use a Vincent V-twin. It was a Norvin which cartoonist Paul Sample decided to be the mount of choice for his 'king of the rockers' creation, Ogri.

But Ogri came in the 1970s, when there was something of a Rocker revival – because by 1965 the Rocker cult had pretty much died its death. Now, the youngsters weren't getting into the bikes in the same manner, as small cars had taken over, while rock and roll was old

One day, one day…

Repairing damaged reputations – a charity 'do' in 1964.

Left: Rocket Gold Star BSA; another favourite machine.

Right: Trip to the south coast seaside, in 1965.

Below: Where to next? Planning a route…

CLASSIC BRITISH LEGENDS 77

hat – replaced by The Beatles, The Stones, The Dave Clark Five, The Troggs et al – and the 1960s was well and truly swinging. Black leather had gone out of fashion (though no-one told Elvis and he sported it for his 1968 comeback in Vegas…) and while there were a few remaining Rockers, most of them were now in their later twenties or older, plenty of them married with children and no longer rocking anything apart from the baby's crib.

Rockers have never completely gone away, there's always been a hardcore, while there were revivals in the mid 1970s and late 80s (Rockabilly led, with Stray Cats etc) but since then, it's been left to the die-hards, really. However, with fashion seemingly being very 1950s led at present, surely it can't be long before the black leather biker jacket makes yet another comeback…

Left: Smartly turned out Norton twin.

Below: Promoting the dream.

LEWIS LEATHERS LTD

UNIVERSAL RACER Mk 2

A waist-length jacket, fully zipped and padded; generously cut (no gap between jacket and breeches). Adjustable wrist and collar. Unique front flap over main zip to keep out dirt & rain; two breast pockets, or single breast pocket and inside pocket - you choose. Suitable for dirt or road use. 100% cotton lined.

Made-to-Measure service at no extra cost.

Available in premium cowhide or veg tanned sheep leather.

WWW.LEWISLEATHERS.COM

Please see our website or visit our central London shop to view more articles from our D Lewis Ltd range
3-5, Whitfield St, London W1T 2SA Tel: 020 7636 4314

Aviakit, D Lewis and Lewis Leathers are trademarks of Lewis Leathers Ltd, 3-5, Whitfield Street, London W1T 2SA Tel: 020 7636 4314

CLASSIC BRITISH
AND EUROPEAN
SILENCERS AND EXHAUST PIPES

You will not find a better product. Armours have made 'HD' quality exhaust systems since 1972. We make them heavy, and use one of the best chromers around. Restorers often tell us that the systems we supplied are still nice after 15 or 20 years' service.

We sell direct to the customer, so our prices are moderate. We send them insured to anywhere in the world. We usually have them in stock for most 1930-1985 models, including

AJS
ARIEL
BSA
DOUGLAS
MATCHLESS
NORTON
PANTHER
ENFIELD
SUNBEAM
TRIUMPH
VELOCETTE
VINCENT

Also available. Two-stroke take-apart silencers, pipes for Villiers engined bikes, plus specials made to customers' old patterns, and

STAINLESS STEEL EXHAUSTS

For pre 85 BMW, Ducati, Laverda, Guzzi, Morini.

Phone quotes and advice with pleasure

CATALOGUE £1 - Lists seats, classic tyres, mudguards, bars, levers, gaskets, harnesses and much more. Catalogue requests taken on card by phone or post.

ARMOURS
www.armoursltd.co.uk
784 Wimborne Road, Bournemouth, Dorset BH9 2HS.
Telephone: 01202 519409. Fax: 01202 510671. Closed Mondays.

"Start a classic journey"

The Classic MotorCycle

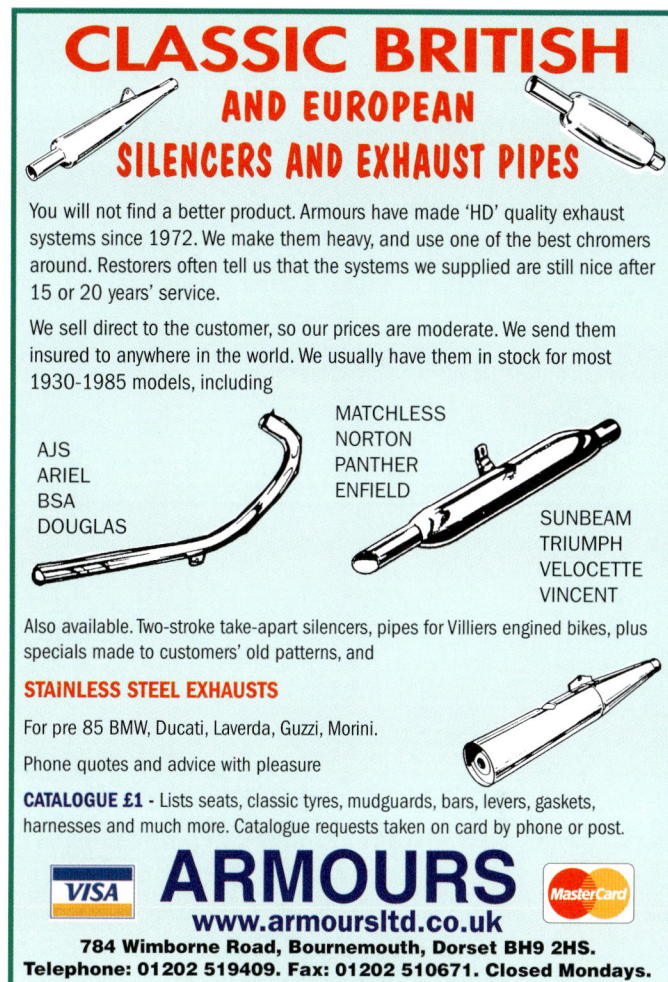

The Classic MotorCycle is the magazine that celebrates motorcycling heritage while remaining firmly rooted in the present. With road tests, features and in-depth stories from the current classic scene, it's a must for the committed classic fan. Pick up a copy today for only £4.10. Available from all good newsagents or direct from Mortons Media Group Ltd.

Call 01507 529529 or visit www.classicmotorcycle.co.uk

Quality Assured

The Mk.VIII KTT – the most handsome motorcycle ever built?

KAMMY CLASS

VELOCETTE KTT

Renowned for the quality of its products, Velocette excelled in international motorcycle racing, culminating in two world championship titles 1949/50, and today is still a force in vintage racing.

Few models have achieved such a long-running level of competitiveness as Velocette's famous KTT, a motorcycle with a competition career which started in the 1920s and lasted well into the 1950s. An interesting detail of KTT-lore is that all KTTs, from the first in 1928 to the last in 1953, run in largely sequential engine numbers, as if to underline the lineage, though admittedly there are several gaps, normally so a new 'mark' can start at an appropriate number; for example, the Mk.IV starts at 401, the last Mk.III being 366.

The first overhead camshaft Velocette engine was designed by Percy Goodman, of the Veloce-founding Goodman family in 1923, though it was 1925 before it made it to production. The early models had 'Veloce' on the petrol tank, but soon this changed to Velocette, as that was the name now recognised by enthusiasts around the world. Prior to the Model K, Veloce had been largely the builder of two-strokes; top quality machines nonetheless, but the first four-stroke (since the company's fledgling years) did mark somewhat of a departure.

Heading to their spiritual home – 'works' Mk.I KTTs heading for the SS Manxman, and the Isle of Man TT races.

However, it was immediately clear the firm was on to a winner – quite literally, for in 1926 Alec Bennett raced his model to victory (incidentally, a 1925 TT bow ended in disappointment, with all three works mounts retiring) and so set in motion a long chain of racing successes for the mark I 'cammy' and its derivatives with other notable wins including TT successes in 1928 (Bennett again) and 1929 (Freddie Hicks).

While the racing led to the KTT (Kamshaft Tourist Trophy – remember, the Goodmans/Guttermans were of German descent!) the Model K was joined by the KSS (for Super Sports) as early as September 1925, though its role as a 'racer' was taken over and it became a fast roadster.

The first production KTT was sold in late 1928, with the mark I continuing through to KTT 266, sold in mid-1930. They were a hit of huge magnitude, being fast, light and, essentially, tough. Specification didn't differ greatly to the KSS though there were some crucial alterations;

Back to where it all began; Alec Bennett, after winning the 1926 TT on the 'cammy' Velo.

Eric Lea, winner of the 1929 Amateur TT (later Manx GP).

strengthening ribs/webs were cast into the crankcase, the revolutionary Harold Willis-designed positive stop gearchange mechanism was fitted and there was extra bracing on the Webb front forks, running from lower fork link brackets to the front wheel hub. Internal engine modifications included improved oiling, a reshaped combustion chamber, high compression piston, double roller big end, larger gudgeon pin and a smaller exhaust valve. It was a racer, pure and simple, capable of upwards of 85mph 'straight from the crate' and 100mph on alcohol fuel

Its potency was demonstrated many times; for example at the 1929 TT 'proper' and Amateur events five KTTs were in the top seven for both races, while in the 1929 Amateur (forerunner to the Manx GP) 500cc Senior race Harold Levings brought his 350cc KTT home second. In the 1930 Manx GP the model's superiority was underlined, Doug Pirie leading home eight Mark I KTTs.

The 1931 season KTTs were called Mk.IIs, but mainly retrospectively and there was very little appreciable difference between them and the Mk.I. Models for 1932 were Mk.IIIs, with only 32 made (the final 14 with four-speed gearboxes), among their altercations being a thicker flange at the cylinder barrel base and a longer neck to the oil filler, to prevent frothing.

For 1933 there was the Mk.IV, officially announced as such (the Mk.II and III had not been 'official') and so the engine

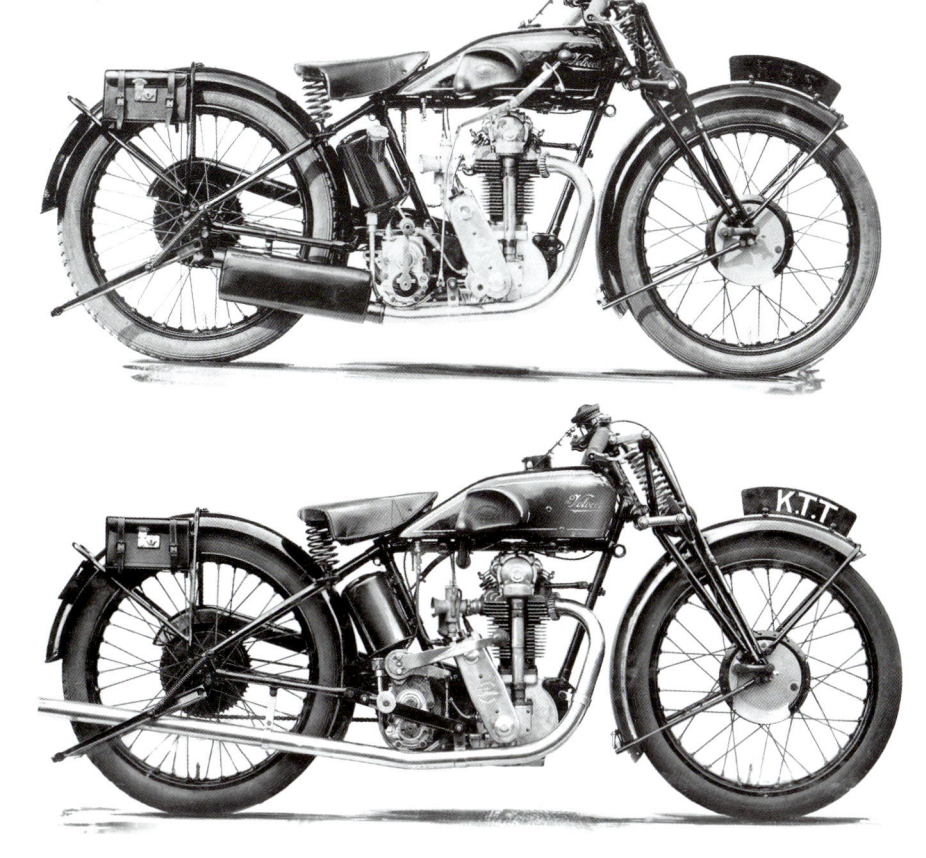

Above: Compare and contrast – the cooking 'cammy,' the KSS, and the racing KTT. Braced forks, foot change, straight through pipe, left side oil filler and no kickstart among variations.

Winner of the 1929 Junior TT, Freddie Hicks, at speed.

CLASSIC BRITISH LEGENDS 83

H E Newman, near Sulby during the 1934 TT.

Life in the old dog yet I; Doug Beasley-framed 250cc (sleeved down) racer, used by Bill Webster. 1953.

Life in the old dog yet II; Geoff Duke's lightweight special, in 1956.

Ted Mellors on the rigid framed racer in the 1936 TT.

The dohc engine; the KTT's ultimate development.

From 1935, the MKV KTT.

number sequence was revised. Main changes included 14mm plug, hairpin valve springs (made under licence from Rudge) and then, from December 1934 being bestowed with a aluminium bronze cylinder head. There were two seasons of Mk.IVs, with 548 the last, in October 1934. The final 50 benefited from the bronze head.

By now, the works racing team was racing machines which were becoming further and further away from the 'production' KTT with different cylinder heads and such on the factory's own models, as well as 500cc options, which were never offered for sale.

The first Mk.V (550) was made in October 1934 – the second and first production one (551) in April 1935. There were 70 Mk.Vs, each with the frame derived from the works racer and bronze cylinder head. Engines were similar to the Mk.IV but with oiling improvements.

Mk.VI KTT is something of an anomaly in that it was an 'official' works

Harry Lamacraft, something of a KTT stalwart, during the 1935 Junior TT.

machine, never to make it to production. It is a fascinating creation though, in that it marked the collaboration (collision…) between 'guru' Willis and star rider Stanley Woods. Willis came up with the engine; a modified Mk.II KSS head (with enclosed valvegear) grafted on to a Mk.V bottom end, while the frame was Woods' influence, with the engine moved forward – Willis always wanted the engine further back, Stanley disagreed…

Only four or five were made, while the original experiment, the 'little rough 'un' was used by Austin Munks to win the 1936 Manx GP.

The MkIV version of the KTT – the final frame development of the old MkI chassis.

The Mk.VIII KTT was probably the first ever 'modern' production racer.

There was now a significant break in KTT production – from the last Mk.V, in late 1935, to the Mk.VII, in early 1938. Meanwhile the works team got on with racing, with dohc engines and swinging arm frames being used, but although it didn't benefit from these advancements, when it came in March 1938 the Mk.VII, despite its rigid frame and single cammy engine, was an otherwise state of the art beauty, once again capable of giving privateers a machine in with a real fighting chance. However, demand wasn't necessarily as expected; just 37 were delivered. Did the buying public have a

Doug Pirie, winner of the 1930 Manx GP.

CLASSIC BRITISH LEGENDS 85

Above: Posing with his Mk.VII at the 1939 TT is G H Hayden.

Below: Racer and author Les Higgins (Mk.VII) and Velo long-time campaigner Tommy Wood (Mk.VIII) during 1947 TT practice.

suspicion of what would come next?

If they did, then surely the Mk.VIII wouldn't have disappointed. Probably the first 'modern' production racer, it was essentially (at a glance, anyway) the machine campaigned by the works for the last couple of years and was available to specially chosen campaigners. There were a few detail differences to the works model campaigned by Stanley W et al (among them the engine finning was nine inch; the works models were 10 inch) but essentially it was the real deal.

Fifty engines had been made before

86 CLASSIC BRITISH LEGENDS

war interrupted proceedings, while the 1939 TT races had truly showcased the model's exceptional nature. There were a whole host entered, with several in the Senior too. The models attracted lots of attention, with the press photographers capturing many images of the speeding machines. Meanwhile, Stanley Woods got on with the winning on a works version. Around 50 (starting at engine number 801) were made by December 1939.

Post Second World War and production restarted in 1947 (at engine number 901), while sales were given

Above: H B Caldwell (fore) and J Garnett, with their KTTs. Caldwell's is one of the first batch of Mk.VIIIs, Garnett's a Mk.VII.

Below: Winning the 1939 Junior TT, is Stanley Woods.

CLASSIC BRITISH LEGENDS

The fastest KTT in the world? Ian Cramp on his super-developed MKI KTT.

Austrian Fritz Binder, who featured in some Veloce sales literature, on the Mk.VII KTT, 1938 Junior race.

Future sidecar world champion Eric Oliver on his Mk.VIII KTT, 1939 Junior TT.

extra boosts by the successes of Bob Foster and Freddie Frith, with Foster winning the 1947 Junior TT, and Frith the 1948 Junior TT, while Grimsby man Frith became the inaugural 350cc word champion in 1949, with 'Fearless' Foster retaining the title for Velocette in 1950. In 1949, Frith rode the 'double knocker' version for many (but not all) races. Alternating when it suited with a special 'big head' single overhead cam model – which apparently gave more torque – Frith won every GP, including the TT. Foster's efforts were particularly praiseworthy, considering that by now the Velocette was becoming seriously outdated, with Norton launching its Featherbed-framed Manx that year. By 1951, the Velos were no longer in the winner's circle.

During the 1950s, KTTs continued to

Runner-up in the 1936 Senior TT – Stanley Woods on the 500cc, spring frame racer; not a KTT strictly, but the lineage is clear.

Freddie Frith winning the 1948 Ulster GP.

be campaigned, while there were a number of 'specials' based upon them, with engines finding their way into lighter, more modern frames. Chief among these were the efforts of Doug St John Beasley, whose 250s (achieved by sleeving down the 350) gave privateers a competitive quarter litre mount.

Later, there was a special Reynolds-framed 350, instigated by no less a man than Geoff Duke and constructed by Reynolds, while stalwarts – such as the famous Arthur Lavington – continued to campaign their KTTs into the 1960s. By the end of that decade, with vintage racing having taken off, the KTTs had a new sphere of competition and, headed by uber enthusiast Ivan Rhodes, set about winning all over again. These days, Ian Cramp's super-developed KTT is one of the fastest 'vintage' machines in the world.

The one and only 600cc 'KTT' engine, built for sidecar driver Stuart Waycott, here being used 'on the grass' at Ringwood in 1951 by Reg Lewis/Gordon Withers.

During the 1948 Swiss GP, impeccable style from Dave Whitworth.

The Nigel Spring equipe at the 1948 TT. Men are Bill Mewis and Jack Bradley.

Bob Foster heads Freddie Frith on the works bikes in 1949.

CLASSIC BRITISH LEGENDS 89

HOME of HEROES

BROOKLANDS

There are few places in Britain which so evoke the spirit of racing heroism as Brooklands. For decades it was at the epicentre of both motor racing and aircraft development. The banked circuit – created by Hugh Locke King, inset above – saw records tumble to men with nerves of steel who were determined to carve out their place in history…

Start of the 1921 Brooklands 500 Miler; 64 starters ready to get under way.

Start of two-lap scratch race, at the first BMCRC meeting, April 1909.

Brooklands race track, in Surrey, was Britain's first purpose built motorsport facility, instigated by Hugh Fortescue Locke King, though greatly assisted by his wife Ethel, who helped bring her husband's dream to fruition and also saved him from bankruptcy.

Hugh was born on October 7, 1848, the son of Peter Locke King, who had inherited a substantial amount of land from his own father and had also been busily buying more too, all in and around Weybridge in Surrey. Peter died in 1885, with the estate, then valued at £500,000, passing to Hugh.

Hugh Locke King was called to the bar in 1873, though it's reckoned he probably never practised. In fact, it seems he really didn't ever have to work for a living, enjoying an opulent lifestyle, which continued in much the same vein, especially after he married Ethel Gore Brown, the youngest daughter of the then governor of Tasmania, later governor of New Zealand. After the death of Locke King Senior, the newlyweds lived at Brooklands House, a mansion built by Peter – at least they did when they were in the country, spending much of their time at their house in Cairo, Egypt.

Among their many passions, the Locke Kings developed a taste for motorsport – and so decided to build a racetrack on their land, the first such purpose built facility in the UK, with the specifications drawn up by Colonel Henry Capel Lofft Holden of the Royal Engineers. Holden, incidentally, had earlier built his own motorcycle. The race track was opened ahead of schedule, in June 1907, with Ethel Locke King (with Hugh as passenger) leading a cavalcade of cars to signify all was ready to go. The task had taken just 10 months.

Early star Frank McNab with his 500cc Trump-JAP, in 1909. He'd just set a new one-hour record, covering 48 miles, 400 yards.

Crowds gather before a race in May 1910.

The first races were held a few days later, although the surface was not finished to the original specification – and never was.

But it was proving much more expensive than had first been envisaged while crowds were not as hoped for – Locke King had thought to attract 30,000 to the first meeting, but just 13,500 showed up. Locke King was raising money as fast as he could, selling or mortgaging almost everything he owned. His health was suffering and for some months Ethel had dealt with his business affairs. She arranged for members of her family to share the debt. At that stage of development

Top: Tommy Green and Cyril Pullin, both Rudge, first and second Brooklands one hour race, October 1913.

Middle: Test Hill, in 1915; Private Read (Indian) enjoys a canter.

Bottom: Handicap race 1914; Brooke's Indian (4) is pushed away, Lauder (6, Henderson four) waits his turn.

Victor Horsman enjoyed much success at the track, first on Norton, then later Triumph.

Bert Le Vack, having won the 1921 500 mile race. Indian's Billy Wells offers his congratulations.

Brooklands had cost, in today's prices, close to £10 million.

The first motorcycle events took place in 1908. Unfortunately, some of the neighbours (who had indeed voiced vociferous opposition during the building process) did not share the Locke Kings' enthusiasm for motor racing and they found sympathetic ears in the courts. Two major court cases resulted in restrictions on track use and enormous claims for damages. At that point, the outer circuit lap record is still somewhat tentatively recorded as belonging to Felicce Nazzaro, an Italian Fiat driver, at 121.64mph – though that figure has forever been questioned. To that point, records of fastest motorcycle lap speeds are impossible to ascertain.

Official racing stopped during the First World War, during the period of which Vickers established its huge factory on the site, after the Locke Kings had offered Brooklands to the Royal Flying Corps. During the war period, it became the centre of aeroplane manufacture in Great Britain, as well as the main flight test centre for the likes of Tom Sopwith and Harry Hawker, among others.

Racing didn't restart at Brooklands

94 CLASSIC BRITISH LEGENDS

Track legend Bill Lacey in his tuning 'shed.' His Grindlay-Peerless stands patiently.

The Brooklands paddock in April 1920.

Joe Wright (1000cc Zenith-JAP) raises the lap record to 117.19mph in April 1929.

until 1920; the reasons were myriad – among them the slow dispersal of the 'fliers' and the poor condition of the track, which had suffered badly from its pounding by army lorries. Racing began on April 5, 1920 – though the full meeting was postponed due to rain but as many had turned up, impromptu match races were organised, among them one pitting Malcolm Campbell's 1912 Lorraine-Dietrich GP car against Jack Woodhouse, on a Motosacoche-engined Matchless. Campbell won.

Lined up on Railway Straight in 1920; unusually, numbers 20 and 22, and the machine behind 20, are all Woolers.

CLASSIC BRITIS LEGENDS 95

Riders start just off the Byfleet Banking, 1923.

In 1921, a motorcycle first exceeded 100mph at Brooklands, thus winning the Godfrey Cup. The man to whom the honour fell was Douglas Davidson, on his V-twin Harley-Davidson – but just two days later Bert Le Vack (Indian) upped the speed to 106.5mph. By now, there was an established group of Brooklands motorcycle habituees – the two mentioned plus others such as Reuben Harveyson, Freddie Dixon and Kaye Don. The outer circuit lap record stood at 94.07mph, to another of the Brooklands regulars, Claude Temple, on a Harley-Davidson.

In 1922, Le Vack (Zenith-JAP) upped the lap record to 100.27mph; the next year Temple (now British Anzani) took it back at 101.23mph, then increased it massively, to 109.94mph in 1924. Joe Wright (Zenith-JAP) was the next man to set the pace – in 1925 he recorded 110.43mph, 113.45 in 1926, then three times in 1929, finishing at 118.86mph in 1929.

Hugh Locke King had been around to see some of Brooklands' 1920s heyday but died, aged 77, in 1926. As the 1920s ended, the circuit record was now held by former AJS works rider Kaye Don who lapped his V12 Sunbeam car at 134.24mph, which was bested by Tim Birkin (Blower Bentley) in 1930, though Don soon had the crown back, raising

Racing stopped during the First World War, during the period of which Vickers established its factory on the site.

The 'new' Campbell Circuit, in 1937. Phil Heath (Vincent) chases Waite and Moss, both Norton.

96 CLASSIC BRITISH LEGENDS

the speed to 137.58mph. It was 1932 before it was raised again.

By the dawn of the 1930s there was a new guard of Brooklands two-wheel heroes, daring stars who fought for track supremacy and broke and rebroke one another's records. Riders such as Bill Lacey, Ted Baragwanath, Ben Bickell, Bert Denly and Chris Staniland were among those who excelled. Staniland actually stopped motorcycle racing at Brooklands during 1930, when he and tuner/entrant 'Woolly' Worters switched their attention to four-wheels, after trade support for two-wheelers at Brooklands was withdrawn.

During the 1930s the Brooklands circuit started to be overtaken for record breaking attempts on tracks such as Montlhery in France, the surface of which was much better. Wright's 1929 lap record was to stand until 1935, when it was bested by Noel Pope (Brough Superior) though later in the year, his like-mounted rival Eric Fernihough went 3mph faster, at 123.58mph. That record stood until 1939, when Pope claimed the all-time motorcycle outer circuit lap record, at 124.51mph.

The four-wheeled record stood at 143.44mph to John Cobb's Napier-Railton, set in 1935, though Chris Staniland, in the Worters-tuned Multi-Union (based on an Alfa Romeo Tipo B), had an all-out attack on it at the August

Two legends of Brooklands – Ben Bickell (Bickell-JAP) leads Dave Whitworth, on his famous, venerable old Blackburne-powered Rex Acme, in 1936.

Riders turn onto the Members Banking, in 1936. Number four is Franics Beart, legendary 1950s and 60s Manx Norton tuner and holder of the Test Hill record.

Bookies at work in 1921.

RAF pilot Chris Staniland, with tuner Woolly Worters and 250cc Rex-Acme Blackburne. He'd just won his race, in 1930, at 90.22mph.

One of the Brooklands heroes. Eric Fernihough, posed outside his Weybridge premises in 1937; he was killed, attempting the motorcycle land speed record in Hungary, in 1938.

Noel Pope wrestles the ex-Baragwanath Brough Superior, to set a new lap record at 127mph, in 1939.

1939 meeting – a misfire meant it was running on only seven cylinders, but Staniland hauled it round at 142.30mph; short of the record, but exceptional nonetheless.

The last motorcycle meeting had already taken place at Brooklands – though those there didn't necessarily know it – on July 15, 1939, when a six race programme was completed. Winners included in the 350cc Junior race Les Archer (Velocette), 500cc Senior race Johnnie Lockett (Norton) while Freddie Clarke used a 501cc Triumph parallel twin to break the 750cc lap record, recording 118.60mph. And so, the track closed in 1939. During the Second World War the site was requisitioned by Vickers, while Wellingtons and Hurricanes were made there. The circuit was covered in camouflage netting, buildings were painted green and brown, a battery of anti-aircraft guns was installed and

Riders ready themselves before the start of a 1934 race.

98 CLASSIC BRITISH LEGENDS

The 1930 Brooklands Grand Prix.

barrage balloons flown overhead. Wellington production at Brooklands ended in 1943 and in the latter years of the war more specialised work was carried out at Brooklands such as the adaptation of Mosquitos to carry a smaller version of Barnes Wallis' bouncing bomb.

Postwar hopes were high that the circuit would reopen – but it never did. Ethel Locke King remained actively involved in the family estates until all the land was eventually sold. She continued to travel up to her death in 1956, when she was 92.

Nowadays, parts of the Brooklands race track remain, including a section of the Byfleet Banking. Attempts to scale it prove just how steep it was. Test Hill remains too, as does the Members Bridge (though it's now a replica) and The Clubhouse. Various replica paddock stalls dot the site, though the Sir Malcolm Campbell shed is the original. The museum boasts a huge display of motorcycles, cars and aeroplane while regular 'running days' see the place a hive of activity – sure, it's not like it was in its heyday, but it's not just the sound of ghosts which reverberate, there's often real, running engines too.

Motorcycles and three wheelers of all sizes line up for the start of the 1935 Hutchison 100.

CLASSIC BRITISH LEGENDS 99

The most famous Duke picture – it encapsulates a new era of the 'first' postwar motorcycle racer. One piece leathers, Featherbed frame... Blandford Camp, Featherbed debut, 1950.

The FIRST POSTWAR MOTORCYCLING SUPERSTAR

GEOFF DUKE
Dominant in the 1950s attaining six world championships, six IoM titles and an OBE to boot – and not forgetting the skintight one piece leathers...

In the years immediately after the Second World War, the British public was crying out for heroes, desperate for some relief after six years of war and continued economic and social problems. Though the war had been won, it had taken a terrible toll on the nation's resources and, ultimately, collective spirit – with things like rationing a daily reminder times were still austere.

So, what was needed was men and women who could make the people's spirits soar, who would bring sunshine and optimism to the lives of the general working public and who would make the British people feel proud to be British. In the motorcycling world, one man ticked more boxes than any other – Geoffrey Ernest Duke.

A familiar sight; picking up the spoils, in Berne, Switzerland, 1952.

CLASSIC BRITISH LEGENDS 101

Trials action, aboard the 500T.

Getting 'psyched up' at Thruxton in 1951.

Born in St Helens, Lancashire, in March 1923, the son of a baker, Geoff's first experience of riding motorcycles came in the mid-1930s, when he and friends would tear about on an early 1920s Raleigh they'd bought between them, though in 1939 Duke bought his first roadster, a 175cc Dot.

By 1942 and with Britain at war, Duke – though in a reserved occupation, working for the Post Office – had enlisted as a dispatch rider, displayed sufficient ability to be retained as an instructor.

Demobbed in 1947, Duke bought a brand new B32 BSA trials iron, soon impressing sufficiently to make the BSA works team, before a 1948 switch to works Nortons, albeit in the trials squad.

But Duke wanted to go road racing; his first race was the 1948 Manx GP, on a 350cc Manx Norton. He was third at the end of lap one and led by lap three… There was disappointment, though, with an engine seizure.

Meanwhile, he was still winning off-road – in both trials and scrambles – but road racing was obviously the future,

In action during the 1949 Clubmans Senior TT.

102 CLASSIC BRITISH LEGENDS

underlined at 1949 Clubman's TT when, on a 490cc Norton 'Inter', Geoff raced to victory, and then double-scored the underlining of his potential by winning the Senior Manx GP, on a 499cc Manx. He was also runner-up in the Junior. Norton had a star on its hands; a place in the 'works' racing team for 1950 was soon confirmed, to nobody's surprise.

Though he was still riding in off-road events – and still doing very well, thank you – 1950 was the year in which Geoff Duke burst upon the scene, becoming that superstar that Britain so eagerly sought. He became a symbol of modernity, of the new postwar order – and he had two key 'props' aiding his way. Number one was his skin-tight one-piece lightweight leather suit, made by St Helens tailor Frank Barker, the second being the Featherbed-framed Manx Norton. For the first time since the end of the war, the image of a man on a racing motorcycle (Duke on his

Having won the 1952 Junior TT, with Norton MD Gilbert Smith. Joe Craig stands by.

Above: Scrapping with the pesky young pretender; Surtees on the inside, Duke wide, at Scarborough in 1955.

Bottom left: On the dustbin faired Gilera in 1957.

Bottom right: Reg Armstrong 'buttons up' – Duke leans on the van.

Featherbed Manx) could not have come from the 1930s; it heralded the dawn of a new era. Geoff Duke was the first modern racing motorcyclist, one of the primary signs in the motorcycle world that times had changed.

Duke got off to winning ways by claiming victory in the 350cc class of the North West 200, won the Senior TT, the Ulster GP and claimed a double at the Italian GP, Monza. He finished the season as runner-up in both 350 and 500cc World Championships; he was just one point adrift from the 500cc title but earlier season tyre troubles – leading to Duke to vow never to race again on Dunlop tyres, a promise he kept – meant he missed out. But he wouldn't have to wait long for world glory. Incidentally, at season's end he took part in the British Experts Trial – he finished fifth against the best trials riders not only in Britain but at that point, the world too.

For the 1951 season Geoff Duke was overwhelmingly the favourite for both 350cc and 500cc titles – he didn't

104 CLASSIC BRITISH LEGENDS

Setting a new 500cc race record, Codogno, Italy.

disappoint, claiming both crowns, which had previously been won by Velocette. Among the factors Duke acknowledged was the work of Leo Kuzmicki, a brilliant engineer who came on board and managed to extract extra power from the Norton engines; for example, in 1950 the 350cc Manx gave 28bhp, in 1951, breathed upon by Kuzmicki, it was up to 36bhp. On the way to title victory came a memorable 350/500cc double in the Isle of Man, while in the 350cc class only a rider's best five results from eight counted; Geoff Duke won five GP. He won four times in the 500cc category. In many ways, that was the pinnacle of Duke's racing career – sure, he went on to win many more races and world

Smart, stylish action through Hilberry on the 350cc Manx.

Tip-toeing round the circuit, at the 1952 Ulster.

Good luck wishes from Stirling Moss.

On a trials BSA, John Douglas Trial, 1953.

CLASSIC BRITISH LEGENDS 105

Above: Aboard the special, swinging arm Ariel Colt in 1957.

Below: Back to where it all began, riding a 'Garden gate' Norton single. This is at Mallory Park VMCC meeting in 1975 – note the footwear!

crowns but in 1951 he was supreme, imperious, the best motorcycle racer in the world, without peer or comparison.

Now a married man, a second 350cc crown followed in 1952, though he wasn't as dominant as he had been, which led some to question whether Duke's moment had passed – though he was still named Sportsman of the Year (basically, the event which evolved into the BBC's Sports Personality of the Year) for his 1951 efforts, in a ballot organised by *The Sporting Record* newspaper, while he had also started racing cars too, with Aston Martin, displaying potential but electing to stick to two wheels. However, an episode at a non-championship race in Schotten is worth noting for it was the only time Duke ever acknowledged that a crash had been the result of his own error. The resulting badly broken ankle finished his season prematurely.

106 CLASSIC BRITISH LEGENDS

Duke approached the 1953 season in something of a quandary – now a businessman with a garage in St Helens, he had choices for 1953; stay with Norton, go to cars, go foreign… The Norton option declined in appeal when Gilbert Smith told Duke a racing four was not a possibility, while a ride on a 350cc Manx in early 1953 re-affirmed his love of two-wheelers over four – and when an offer from Gilera (in fact, there had been earlier offers too) materialised, it was to them his allegiance switched. Now an OBE, Duke was soon entrenched at Gilera – and after a early 'clash' or two, he found the Gilera people receptive to his changes and they set about building a race winning, near unbeatable, four-cylinder mount. Wins on the 500 in Holland, France, Switzerland and Italy were harvested on his way to the 500cc title.

In 1951 Duke was supreme, imperious, the best motorcycle racer in the world, without peer or comparison.

Redesign followed for 1954, resulting in a Gilera with which Duke won even more comfortably, the end note being another world championship and several memorable victories, chief among them being beating a grid full of pumped up Italians in their home GP. The world crown was duly delivered.

Next year there were more wins, including in the Senior TT, and the third consecutive 500c world crown, but the most notable development of the season was what transpired at the Dutch TT when Geoff's support of a privateers' protest at the lack of start money (12 riders in the 350cc class pulled in at the end of lap one) led to Duke receiving a worldwide ban stretching till July 1956; it was relented to allow Duke to ride in

Top: The start of a winning combination, winning the 1953 GP Des Nations in Italy.

Middle: Try out on a Manx, in 1958.

Bottom: Back on a Gilera in the Isle of Man; a parade lap in 1973.

CLASSIC BRITISH LEGENDS 107

some non-championship events, but it ensured there was to be no fourth consecutive world crown and, it proved, no more world crowns at all.

The 1957 season was miserable, ruined by injuries, chief among them a dislocated shoulder, and then at the end of the year, Gilera quit; Duke though elected to struggle on, though with hindsight he recognised it would perhaps have been beneficial to his legacy to have called it a day. Thing was, he still enjoyed his racing.

Above: A late race outing.

Right: With a BMW Rennsport, 1958 Senior TT.

A new lightweight 350cc Norton was built, with Ken Sprayson of Reynolds making the frame, while in the 500cc class Geoff secured the use of a 500cc Rennsport BMW. The season was up and down, never hitting earlier heights, with the highlight a 350/500cc double at the Swedish GP, though the 500cc race victory was achieved on a Norton. The BMW was retired in the Senior TT.

There were a few appearances after, culminating in a final meeting – a non-championship Swiss race in September. And Duke didn't disappoint, winning three races on a works 250cc Benelli, his lightweight 350cc Norton and a standard 500cc Manx. And so the curtain was drawn on an illustrious career.

Geoff Duke wasn't done with racing – he ran Scuderia Duke with the 1957 Gileras recommissioned in 1963, while he was also involved with Royal Enfield and its 250cc GP5.

Having moved to the Isle of Man in the 1950s, it was there Geoff Duke retired too, becoming a hotelier and running the successful Duke Video enterprise.

Top: Unmistakeable, poetry in motion... Duke and Gilera, 1955.

Above: Heavy landing with the 'Duke Special' Norton in the 1959 Junior TT; a fourth place finish resulted.

Frank Applebee, winner of the 1912 TT.

SILKY SMOOTH these SCOTTS

THE SCOTT MOTORCYCLE
One of the first companies to use water cooling in its motorcycles, Scott gained rapid success taking several TT wins and numerous lap records...

Founder of the Scott motorcycle company was a Mr Alfred Angas Scott. A highly intelligent and free thinking man, Scott was educated at, among other places, Abbotsholme school near Uttoxeter, which is where, every year, the owners club now holds its annual rally. Born in Bradford in 1874, Alfred Scott was schooled both in Scotland and then, for his final year, at Abbotsholme. Fiercely self reliant, he never did things in a straightforward and orthodox way – hence his motorcycles. A trained engineer, the first Scott motorcycles were up and running – and competing, and winning, in competition – by 1908, with a first advert appearing in *The Motor Cycle* in 1909. The early models (with two cylinders, two-stroke, two gears and water cooling) were by no means perfect – but they were pretty good. In the pre-First World War period Scott went from strength to strength, culminating in successive TT wins in 1912 and 1913 and fastest laps every year 1911-14. Victor in 1912 was Frank Applebee, while the 1913 victory was achieved courtesy of rider 'Tim' (short for 'Timber' – his older brother was 'Splinters' hence the younger was 'Timber', Tim for short – though his real name was Harold) Wood, a Bradford native and long time Scott employee.

Almost the pinnacle; a 1922 model two-speed Scott.

CLASSIC BRITISH LEGENDS

'Timber' Wood, who raised the lap record to 52.12mph in the 1913 TT.

Scott sidecar with new suspension, in 1912.

The then 22-year-old's remarks on his training regime are 'illuminating' – "I was teetotal and refrained from smoking for a week then gave it up in disgust. I simply went in for plenty of sleep and it served me well."

By the end of the First World War, Alfred Scott had seemingly lost enthusiasm for motorcycles – he sold his shares in his eponymous company in December 1918. He established another business to build what he was now interested in; the three-wheeled Scott Sociable.

Meanwhile, motorcycle manufacture continued, but no longer was Scott the great innovator – there was nothing new or groundbreaking, with the same two-speed models being marketed year in, year out. By the mid-1920s they were long in the tooth to say the least, with frames and cycle parts that really were indistinguishable from the veteran period models.

Mr W Fawcett, with his Scott, at Harrogate in 1910.

112 CLASSIC BRITISH LEGENDS

Alfred Angas Scott, at the controls of his Sociable.

Scott Sociable, a cross between the sidecar and motorcar.

Meanwhile, Alfred Angas had died in 1923 (incidentally, the first year the 'Squirrel' name was coined for a Scott), contracting pneumonia after driving home, wet, from a potholing expedition, in his Sociable. The Sociable itself went out of production in 1925.

By the mid-1920s, though Scott had a loyal hardcore of enthusiasts, the company was acutely aware it needed to broaden its motorcycles' appeal, to make them more accessible. A three-speed gearbox had been offered since 1923, but this was just fitted to the standard model, and retained the open frame and 'biscuit barrel' petrol tank, beloved of Scottists, but viewed as curios by the non-believers.

So, what was needed was a model of more regular appearance – so (re)enter the Flying Squirrel; the name had actually been used before, for a fast two-speeder.

But to the newcomer, which was to be arguably Scott's most important and famous model. Drawing heavily on the 1926 TT practice, the new duplex frame was actually of standard (and sound)

Machine gun carrier, in 1914.

114 Classic British Legends

1: Towing out a Flying Flea, in 1926.

2: The depot at the 1921 TT.

3: Relaxing in the depot, before the 1925 Senior.

4: So this is Yorkshire; the Scott Trial, 1925.

Left: Clarrie Wood pushes on, despite the muddy conditions, in 1923.

Scott practice, utilising triangles for their strength, though rather than the open manner of previous Scotts, the frame on the 'Flyer' – which was also appreciably heavier than the earlier efforts – had a top tube which was bolted in place and contained within the petrol/oil tank. Forks too were a development of what had gone before, though were greatly strengthened with more 'triangles' added.

What was needed was a model of more regular appearance – enter the Flying Squirrel.

On its launch, the new model was greeted enthusiastically, almost ecstatically, by the Press. Both *The Motor Cycle* and *Motor Cycling* seem to have been staffed by dedicated fans of the Shipley maker, which can't have done the prospect of sales any harm at all. And help would be needed – on launch in late 1926 the Flying Squirrel was phenomenally expensive, at upwards of £90, with more for the 600cc version.

In what can only really be described as an 'ecstatic' April 1928 road test, the tone is set from the beginning. "Being a Pressman has its compensations, and to have to road-test a Scott is decidedly one of them. Nobody can claim to have known every joy of motorcycling until they have ridden the 1928 model Flying

CLASSIC BRITISH LEGENDS **115**

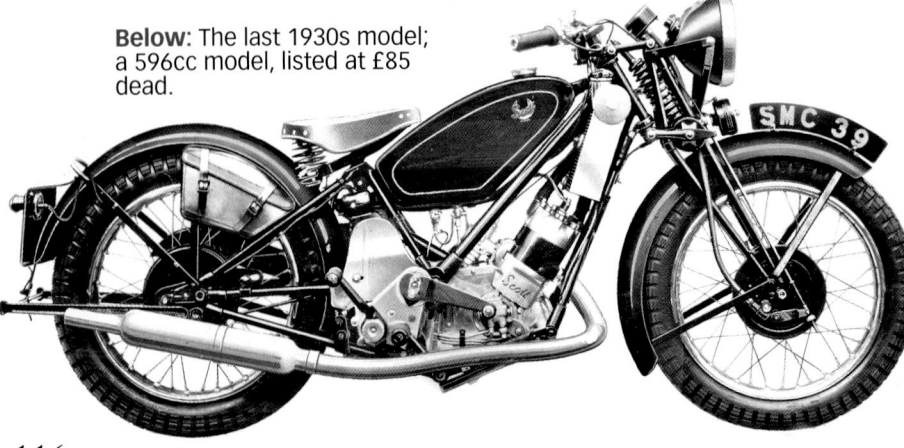

Below: Liverpool-based Scott stalwart and Albert Reynolds built some luxurious specials in the 1930s – this one dates to 1932.

Below: The Dirt Track racer. Frank Varey (aka 'The Red Devil') enjoyed particular success aboard one.

Below: Scott inline triple – it was listed for several years, but few were made.

Below: The last 1930s model; a 596cc model, listed at £85 dead.

Squirrel on a cross-country journey."

Problem was, it was still extremely expensive and by 1929 Scott was acutely aware of this. The Flying Squirrel De Luxe kept the Scott forks, but the new Flying Squirrel Tourer was added, which featured a few cost cutting measures, including the use of Webb forks and cheaper wheels. This meant it was possible to sell the 500cc model at £67-10s; still expensive, but at least it made it more accessible.

There was also the TT Replica; based on the model which Tommy Hatch used to finish third in the 1928 Senior TT, and introduced in late 1928, the TT Replica is considered by many the best of the 'heavy' Scotts. Boasting such go-faster goodies as big-bore Siamese exhaust, cylinder wall oiling fed from the rear of the block, quick fillers on the petrol tank and ribbed rear brake drum, it offered a new level of performance. It also introduced many of the features – the shortened frame and the longer stroke engine – which were to find their way on to the cooking Flying Squirrels.

By 1930, the TT Replica was listed alongside the Flying Squirrel De Luxe and the Flying Squirrel Tourer. Scott's press release described it as combining '…the touring comfort and reliability of the De Luxe Scott with great speed and safety' and also notes it as being capable of 'serious racing work.'

Having been mildly critical the year before of a Flyer and sidecar, *The Motor Cycle* rhapsodised about the Flying Squirrel Tourer and it proved popular. Indeed, Scott issued a statement accompanying and introducing its 1930 range, which has remained in our archive;

"In consequence of the really competitive prices established last year, Scott motor cycles have enjoyed an

Above: Bernal Osbourne tests the 500c prototype, with flat-top pistons, in 1958. It was apparently good for more than 90mph.

116 CLASSIC BRITISH LEGENDS

unprecedented wave of popularity and sales have shown, in the 1929 season, the astonishing advance of more than one hundred and twenty per cent". Scott added the underlining themselves.

Still, it sold – and it sold well, which was a good job, as other ventures – such as the 300cc two-stroke single – failed a) to convince or b) sell in any meaningful numbers.

In 1931, there was a change in frame design for the Flying Squirrel, with the old twin downtube design giving way to a single front and saddle tube effort, which owed much to the popular 1930 Sprint Special. By now, Scott was in one of what was to become regular times of financial difficulties – an official receiver

Top: Another failure... The new TT racer, with vertical cylinder barrels.

Left: Show-stopper – but never produced. Vertical cylinder 650cc twin at Earls Court in 1930.

The ill fated 300cc air-cooled single, 1930.

CLASSIC BRITISH LEGENDS **117**

The 1921 TT - R W Stansfield, on his two-speed racer.

was appointed and with his appointment, so went any prospect of the new 650cc engine for the Flyers. Also, the open-framed two-speed models were finally discontinued.

By the 1930s, Scott was now in what is viewed with hindsight as a downward spiral; actually, even at the time it must have been apparent. Gone were the light and lithe Squirrels of the roaring 1920s and every year, the Squirrel became less Flyer, more 'fatter.'

There were updates and upgrades, but by 1934 there was just the Flying Squirrel Tourer, De Luxe and Replica left available as 500 or 600cc models. Despite a three-cylinder job being built and even road tested by the Press it never made it to volume production though it was listed – alongside just the Flying Squirrel – from 1935 onwards. The Squirrel continued, with plunger suspension offered, while there was also in 1939 a new model, the tuned Clubman's Special, with a 90mph guarantee, thanks to its heavily tuned engine. Thing was, though, like the Squirrels, it was carrying far, far too

The seventh production Silk is collected by its owner, Mr M N Morris of Greenhithe, Kent.

118 CLASSIC BRITISH LEGENDS

From 1949, little changed from before the war, but with telescopic forks.

Pictured in January 1972, a Silk-Scott, with Scott engine.

much weight. Scotts had become rather more sedentary sloths than nimble scurriers and during the period 1931-40 Scott had made 1356 motorcycles – in 1929 alone they had made 1398.

After the Second World War, production restarted in 1946/47 with an updated version of the prewar job – basically, the same, (with girder forks) but then with the addition of Dowty Oleomatic telescopic forks which, if nothing else, modernised the look of the Scotts. But it was to little avail – the company was struggling badly and entered voluntary liquidation in 1950.

Scott was bought by Aerco Jig Company, with everything moved to Birmingham; by now, no machines were being built. A prototype with an all new duplex swinging arm frame appeared in 1954 though it was 1956 before it was announced production had re-started, with the Flying Squirrel the only model offered. A new machine, the Swift, was developed, but never made it to production.

The Flying Squirrel continued to be made in limited numbers into the early 1960s, while in the 1970s came the Silk, the natural successor.

An attempted comeback. Matt Holder (left) and Brian Woolley (right) with the Scott 350cc racer. Rider Barry Scully is suitably togged up.

No LIGHTWEIGHT PERFORMER

BSA BANTAM
With over 400,000 built, the BSA Bantam was many a rider's first foray on powered two wheels.

Under economy testing in Australia, 1950. A massive 213mpg was attained.

The most famous 'working' motorcycle ever made, certainly in Britain? The BSA Bantam is close, if not the one. Sure, it's not possessed of the glamour of its Gold Star stablemate or the Triumph Bonneville, but the little BSA was known intimately and ridden extensively by a whole lot more riders than those two put together. And the story for this most British of legends all began in Germany. In the aftermath of the Second World War, the Allies plundered the broken Fatherland for repatriations and one of the spoils was the DKW factory's neatly styled and soundly designed RT125 model. Manufacturers around the world (including Harley-Davidson and later Yamaha) produced versions of the German engine, but in Britain, BSA's Bantam, launched in 1948, became the best-selling variant; by 1953, 100,000 had already been sold. The original engine for the 123cc D1 (the first of the line) was a mirror image of the German design, fitted into basic but strong cycle parts. The first rigid-framed offerings, with simple telescopic front fork and painted wheels, offered cheap, dependable and modern looking ride-to-work machines for a country desperately trying to recover from the war.

Bond girl Mollie Peters (*Thunderball*) seems impressed by the young man's Bantam Supreme...

A familiar sight in 1950s and 60s Britain – an L-plate bedecked Bantam.

District nurses with their Bantams in Australia, 1951.

BSA even sold a Competition version of that early D1 Bantam with trials tyres, high clearance front mudguard and upswept exhaust, starting the off-road career of many an aspiring mud-plugger. The basic, base-model D1 Bantam acquired chrome wheel rims in 1954 and options such as plunger rear suspension and even a dual seat and pillion footrests as time went by. The low seat height and modest weight made the Bantam easy to handle, while the fact they weren't all black seemed to encourage potential new riders too. Maintenance was basic and clearly explained, while rider training schemes adopted them too, and a D1 Bantam was the first powered two-wheeler for many a rider.

Though the D1 was the mainstay of the range for many years, BSA continued to develop the basic model, with the 150cc D3 Major for 1954 the first update. The engine capacity hike was achieved by a hike in the cylinder bore size, from the D1's 52mm to 57mm, while retaining the same stroke (58mm) as the littler offering. This extra 25cc pushed power up from 4.5bhp to 5.3bhp which in reality equated to a 45mph, rather than 40mph for the D1, realistic cruising speed. For the new model the forks were beefed up too while all three versions of the newcomer (direct lighting, battery

Easy does it; Bantam balancing, 1950.

Above: The Bushman, pictured in 1969.

122 CLASSIC BRITISH LEGENDS

The 50,000th Bantam comes off the line, May 1951.

lighting and Competition) featured the sprung frame and were finished in a pastel grey coating all over, relieved by cream tank panels.

The new model made its public 'bow' alongside the 100,000th D1 Bantam made, both at the centre of BSA's stand at Earls Court in late 1953. The D3 continued on, developed along the way, gaining a modern swinging arm frame in 1956, while there were new colours too, with maroon among them.

Of course, no Bantam story is complete without mention of the GPO (General Post Office) Bantams, with over 6500 supplied for use by the service's telegram boys, the first batch of which were supplied in the last month of 1948; interestingly, these were painted the standard mist green, but soon, the familiar all-over red finish became

The same 'line worker' is supervised by a group from the Western African distributor, G B Ollivant Ltd.

Brenda Collins in New York, at the end of her 10,000 mile US, Canada and Mexico tour.

CLASSIC BRITISH LEGENDS 123

Two above: The 125cc D1 and the more obviously modern 175c D7.

standard issue. During the 1960s when private telephone ownership became ever more common, so the necessity for telegrams negated, meaning less and less Bantams were used. The vast majority of those supplied had been D1s, in rigid and plunger form, though at the death (in 1971), the last few were B175s.

The first of those several 175cc models, which eventually led to the final B175 and of which all had swinging-arm rear suspension, came late in 1957 in the shape of the briefly listed D5, while in February 1957, the 150,000th Bantam was produced. But the new D5 offered a more modern motorcycle all round, with its smaller 18inch wheels and a bulkier petrol tank, allied to the D3's swinging arm frame, allowing it to look really quite current.

That modern look was further enhanced with 1959's D7; this truly was a miniature version of the 'bigger bikes' in BSA's range, in particular the newly

Speed testing – the brute power examplred...

124 CLASSIC BRITISH LEGENDS

introduced, unit construction 250cc C15. Indeed, the D7 actually featured a shorter version of the C15's forks, as well as toolboxes/side panels, seat and headlamp nacelle, all a la the bigger models. The frame was all-new too and overall, the Bantam had become a much more modern looking machine, even over the D5, which itself had been quite a step. The engine was little changed from the D5, with 7.5bhp the claimed power output.

Despite all the incarnations and modifications, meanwhile the basic D1 soldiered on to help the Bantam become BSA's best-selling motorcycle. After a 15-year run, it was finally dropped from the catalogue in 1963.

In 1964, the basic D7 was joined by a De Luxe model – though there was little sign of that fourth cog in the gearbox which all agreed was what the baby BSA most urgently needed. Styling touches were added, different versions of the basic D7 came about and the D7 struggled on. It wasn't until late 1966 when a four-speeder finally made its bow in the racy-looking (humped back seat, flyscreen, upswept pipe, chequer tape on tank) D10S, although the other 'new'

Sheep minding duties in the Australian outback.

D10s (such as the Super and the no-frills economy Silver) still had the old three speed gearbox. The Bushman soon made its debut too, itself benefiting from a four-speed gearbox; arguably the first 'trailie' motorcycle, the majority of the 3500 made went abroad. But it, and the Sports version, proved that there was perhaps a little life left in the old bird yet.

Soon, the D10 ceded to the D14/4; the four signalling that all models now had the four-speed gearbox but by now it was 1968 and the change had come five, or probably 10, years too late… Power was up too, with 13bhp claimed, about 12.5bhp more likely – but superstition led to the non-use of the '13' designation. Whatever, the Bantam could

Top: You will come for a ride on my Bantam, you will, you will…

Left: Well laden from the options catalogue in 1966.

now (hills and headwinds accepted…) cruise at 60mph – or thereabouts.

There were Bushman and Sports versions of the D14 too, while there was one last incarnation of the Bantam to come – the April 1969-announced B175. Triumph Cub forks were fitted, but otherwise it was fairly like what had gone before, though that was not necessarily a bad thing; indeed, it was widely reckoned to be one of, if not the, best of the Bantams. So at least BSA had learned something, with the last being the best, though by 1970 even the best Bantam couldn't really keep with what else was on offer, mainly those machines from the Orient. By March 1971 the Bantam was discontinued; over 400,000 had been

Top: BSA was fond of Bond girls; this is Caron Gardner, at Earls Court in 1964.

Right: Bantam earns its keep in 1963.

BSA 125 c.c. Two-stroke Model D1 Competition

The competition Bantam.

Sales illustration for the Bushman.

made and for the most part it had been a long, proud if perhaps occasionally stubborn innings.

All through its life, and to this day, people searched out ways to make the Bantam go faster and perform competitively in sporting events. The BSA works played with it, the likes of Johnny Draper, Brian Stonebridge and Brian Martin appearing sporadically aboard special Bantams in the 1950s, then Mick Bowers and Dave Rowland enjoying some trials success in the 1960s. Many were road raced too, both at home and abroad, within the UK the Hogan brothers John and Peter and George Todd at the forefront, while in Australia Eric Walsh was the man who tuned a streamlined Bantam to achieve 115mph before ignition troubles prevented higher speeds. Probably the greatest sporting achievement was Fred Launchbury's 20th place in the 1967 125cc TT, aboard a Todd breathed upon ex-GPO Bantam. He

BSA 175 c.c. SILVER BANTAM

Above: From 1966, the Silver Bantam.

Right: A flyscreen. Oh yes.

Late Bantam 175, tastefully adorned.

averaged a touch under 74mph.

Meanwhile, Bantam racing had taken off in the 1960s as a cheap and accessible form of motorsport – and continues to be well-supported, with super-developed Bantams going at it hammer and tongs in their series, run with the VMCC's British Historic Racing arm. Elsewhere, Bantams have come into vogue in pre-65 trials, with much modified examples now among the machines to beat.

Bantams continue to offer dependable service to many riders, though few are used as 'ride-to-work' machines today.

Early D1s remain the most popular, their cheeky, quirky looks and diminutive stature meaning they are still the source of much pleasure, while later Bantams – particularly the four-speed versions – offer good, honest classic fun at an affordable price.

D10 Sports Bantam, with four-speed gearbox, in 1966.

Under instruction in 1965.

CLASSIC BRITISH LEGENDS 129

VINTAGE & VETERAN

PURVEYORS OF FINE MOTORCYCLES

WE ARE PRIVILEGED TO BE INSTRUCTED TO OFFER THESE ICONIC MACHINES FOR SALE - ALL REASONABLE OFFERS WILL BE CONSIDERED - SEE WEBSITE FOR MORE DETAILED PHOTOS AND A DESCRIPTION

Ring Phil Haywood or Ken Ashton to discuss any machine - we buy and sell for cash settlement - with discretion

www.vinandvet.com

Vintage and Veteran LLP, 17 Studio 1, Waterside Court, Third Ave, Burton on Trent DE14 2WD • +44 (0) 1283 509 562 • email vinandvet@aol.com